Master a Career-Defining Skill in 90 Days:

A Proven Framework for Growth, Confidence, and Success

DAN CLAPPER

DEDICATION

To those who refuse to settle,
Who dream beyond boundaries,
And who rise, again and again, in pursuit of their better selves.

For every moment you doubted your path but kept going anyway,
For every lesson learned through struggle,
And for every small victory that brought you closer to your dreams.

I've been where you are, standing at the edge of possibility, unsure
of what comes next.

But I can tell you this—growth is always within your reach,
And the potential inside you is far greater than you realize.

Never stop believing in your ability to achieve greatness.

CONTENTS

ACKNOWLEDGMENTS

This work would not have been possible without the unwavering support and encouragement of those around me. To my family, for their love, patience, and belief in me throughout this journey — thank you for being my foundation.

I am deeply grateful to my friends, mentors, and colleagues, whose insights, feedback, and encouragement have been invaluable. Your contributions have shaped both this project and my growth along the way.

A special and heartfelt thanks to the incredible medical professionals who guided me through my heart attack and brain hemorrhage this summer. Your expertise, care, and compassion gave me a second chance at life, and for that, I will forever be grateful. You have not only restored my health but also rekindled my purpose to give back to the world.

1
YOUR JOURNEY STARTS HERE

Have you ever felt stuck in your career—pushing hard but seeing no progress?

That feeling of being trapped in the same routine, waiting for something—anything—to change can be overwhelming. You're not alone. This frustration, this "career stuckness," is something almost everyone faces at some point in their professional lives.

I know because I've been there. There were times I doubted myself, questioned my potential, and wondered if I'd ever break free from the cycle. I worked harder, took on more responsibilities, and still found myself asking, *Why isn't this working?*

The truth is effort alone isn't enough. To grow, build confidence, and achieve success, you need more than just hard work—you need a proven framework.

Introducing the FASST Career Growth Framework

That's why I created this book. It's not just a collection of ideas or theories; it's a step-by-step guide to help you find clarity, take control, and move forward with purpose. The FASST Career Growth Framework is the result of years of trial and error, research, personal breakthroughs, and professional achievements. It's designed to give you the tools to:

- **Achieve Growth:** Break through barriers and create meaningful momentum in your career.

- **Build Confidence:** Understand your strengths, overcome self-doubt, and embrace your potential.

- **Experience Success:** Define what success looks like for you and take intentional steps to make it a reality.

Unlike generic advice or quick-fix solutions, this framework focuses on actionable steps tailored to your unique challenges. Having encountered much of the overhyped, surface-level advice out there, I knew I had to build something different—something grounded in measurable results.

The FASST Career Growth Model is practical, actionable, and tailored to meet you where you are right now. It will guide you to:

- **Find Your Fire:** Discover the passion and drive that fuels growth.

- **Assess Honestly:** Evaluate your current situation with clarity and honesty.

- **Optimize Skills and Support Systems:** Sharpen your abilities and build a network that empowers you.

- **Master Time:** Focus on what matters most and align your efforts with your goals.

A Journey of Transformation

Picture this journey as a winding path leading to a bright horizon. You can start exactly where you are, and along the way, you'll encounter milestones representing your growth.

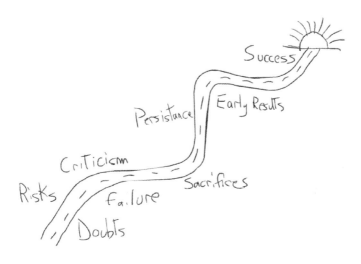

Imagine this: 90 days from now, you're looking back at a period of incredible growth. You feel more confident in your abilities, clearer about your direction, and genuinely excited about the path you're on. That's what's possible when you embrace this framework and commit to the process.

How to Make the Most of This Book

Reading this book is just the first step in mastering a career-defining skill. Real transformation happens when you actively engage with the material. The strategies outlined here are actionable steps designed to produce measurable results. To help you truly benefit, I've integrated three types of interactive elements throughout the book:

Self-Reflection Questions

At the end of each chapter, you'll find thought-provoking questions to help you internalize the material. These prompts encourage you to reflect on how the concepts apply to your unique circumstances, serving as a foundation for your growth.

3

- **Here's your Self-Reflection Question for this chapter:** What does "career stuckness" mean to you? Have you experienced this feeling before? Describe a specific instance.

 ### Immediate Action Steps

Each chapter includes practical, actionable tasks to implement what you've learned. This is where theory becomes progress. Commit to completing these exercises—your future self will thank you.

- **Immediate Action Step for this chapter:** Write down three reasons why you feel "stuck" in your career and one small action you can take today to begin addressing each reason.

 ### Prompts to Share with Your Peer Network

Growth is magnified when shared with others. Engage with a peer network, accountability partner, or online community to reinforce your commitment and gain valuable feedback.

- **Here's your prompt to share for this chapter:** Share your reflections or action plan with a trusted accountability partner or post them in an online community like The Top 10% Club. Ask for feedback on your ideas and suggestions for additional actions you might take.

Your Success Starts with Action

This book isn't just something to read—it's a guide to do. Reflect deeply, take bold action, and connect with others. If you do, you won't just master a career-defining skill—you'll create lasting change in your career and life.

Commit to this journey, and in 90 days, you won't just be dreaming of a better career—you'll be living it.

Cheers to a great start!

Your Friend, Dan

2
WHY THE 90 DAY FRAMEWORK CHANGES EVERYTHING

What if I told you that in just 90 days, you could master a skill that transforms your career—and your confidence?

Congratulations on taking the first step toward achieving exactly that. By deciding to engage with this framework, you've already set yourself apart from most professionals who remain stuck in cycles of vague goals and unstructured growth. You're proving that you're ready for intentional change.

If you're anything like me, you've probably had a skill you've wanted to master for months, maybe even years. You've read articles, attended seminars, or squeezed practice into your packed schedule. But progress might have felt slow, scattered, or unsatisfying. Sound familiar?

You're not alone. Most of us struggle to find the time and structure to make real progress. That's why this 90-day framework is a game-changer—it's designed for busy professionals like you who want practical, measurable results without overhauling their entire lives.

Why This Framework Works

The 90-day framework is built around three core principles:

Clear, Actionable Steps

Each step is practical and to the point, so you can immediately apply it to your daily life. The focus is on doing, not just thinking.

Consistency Over Complexity

Instead of relying on big, dramatic efforts, this framework emphasizes small, consistent actions that compound over time to deliver meaningful results.

Results You Can Measure

By the end of 90 days, you'll see tangible improvements in your chosen skill—outcomes that matter in your career, whether it's greater efficiency, increased confidence, or recognition from others.

This method respects the reality of your busy life. It empowers you to integrate skill-building seamlessly into your routine. Imagine what's possible when growth becomes part of your everyday life.

Designed by Default vs. Designed with Intention

Most of us approach skill-building by default. It often looks like this:

- **Sporadic Efforts:** Attending a one-off seminar, reading a random article, or practicing inconsistently.

- **No Clear Plan:** Without a strategy, progress is slow and often frustrating.

- **Fading Motivation:** Enthusiasm wanes, and without reinforcement, skills are rarely applied or retained.

Now, compare that to a 90-day framework, which is designed with intention:

- **Frequent, Focused Learning Sessions:** Dedicating just 5-20 minutes at a time builds momentum and compounds your knowledge.

- **Consistent Progress:** Incremental improvements lead to steady, meaningful growth.

- **Staying Engaged:** A clear, time-bound goal keeps you motivated and focused.

Which approach sounds more effective to you?

Why 90 Days?

Ninety days is the sweet spot for mastering a skill. It strikes a perfect balance between being long enough to create meaningful results and short enough to stay motivating. In three months, you'll have the time to dive deeply into new concepts, refine your techniques, and apply what you've learned to real-world situations.

This consistent practice reinforces retention and builds confidence, helping you not only to develop your skill but also to feel genuinely capable in applying it.

Shorter timeframes, like 30 days, often feel rushed and leave little room for habit formation or significant progress. On the other hand, committing to an entire year can feel overwhelming and lead to a loss of focus.

Ninety days gives you just the right amount of time to set a clear goal, make steady progress, and see measurable outcomes—whether it's increased efficiency, greater recognition, or enhanced confidence. By the end of this period, you'll have real, tangible results to show for your efforts.

Imagine the Possibilities

Think of it like building a snowball. Each small action adds to the momentum until you've created something truly impactful. By the end of 90 days, you won't just feel more skilled—you'll have the confidence to take on bigger challenges and the proof that your efforts lead to success.

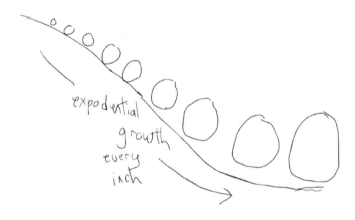

Each roll of the snowball represents your daily effort. With each push, your progress builds on itself, creating unstoppable momentum.

This framework isn't about theory—it's about action. Now it's time to start building your momentum. Commit to the next 90 days as a transformative period in your life. Small, consistent efforts will lead to incredible results.

Self-Reflection Question

What skill have you struggled to master in the past, and what has held you back? How do you think the 90-day framework could address those obstacles?

 **Immediate Action Step**

Start brainstorming a list of skills that you would like to master. Dream big. Don't limit yourself— write down anything that excites or inspires you. We will dive deeper in the next chapter on how to choose the right skill.

 **Prompt to Share with Your Peer Network**

Share your brainstorming list of skills with a trusted accountability partner or in an online community like The Top 10% Club. Invite them to share their ideas as well and discuss what excites you most about these possibilities. Their insights might spark new ideas or help you refine your focus as you prepare for the next chapter.

3
CHOOSING THE RIGHT SKILL TO MASTER

What if the next skill you choose to master could transform your career?

The right choice has the power to boost your confidence, accelerate your growth, and open doors to new opportunities. Choosing the right skill to master is the foundation of your 90-day journey. It's the decision that defines your focus, shapes your growth, and ultimately determines the impact you'll make in your career.

Get this right, and the path ahead becomes clear. Get it wrong, and you risk spinning your wheels on something that doesn't move you forward.

It's easy to get stuck when deciding where to focus. You might feel overwhelmed by all the possibilities or second-guess whether the skill you're choosing is the "right" one. But don't worry—this chapter will guide you through a simple, effective framework to decide with confidence.

Mistakes to Avoid When Choosing a Skill

Before we dive into the framework, let's address a few common traps that can derail your decision-making:

One common mistake is choosing a skill out of weakness. It's tempting to focus on what you're bad at, but not all weaknesses are worth fixing. The best skills to master are those that align with your strengths and bring real value to your work.

Another pitfall is ignoring relevance. Picking a skill that doesn't connect to your current role or future aspirations can lead to frustration and wasted effort. Instead, stay aligned with what matters most to you and your career goals.

Finally, don't fall into the trap of chasing trends without strategy. Trendy skills might seem appealing, but if they don't excite you or fit your goals, they'll quickly lose their luster. The key is choosing a skill that matters now and will continue to matter in the future.

So how do you make the right choice? By finding the sweet spot where three critical elements overlap: Exciting, Practical, and Impactful.

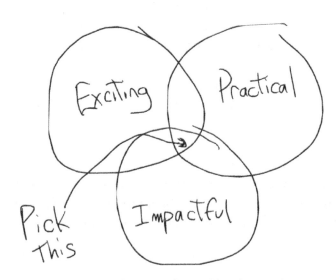

The Sweet Spot: Exciting, Practical, and Impactful

Think of this as a Venn diagram with three circles. The skill you're looking for lies at the intersection of these three elements:

- **Exciting:** Start by choosing a skill that sparks your curiosity and creativity. Think about activities that make you lose track of time because you enjoy them so much. Excitement is your fuel—when you're genuinely excited about a skill, you're unstoppable.

- **Practical:** Next, consider how this skill addresses a current challenge or problem in your life or work. A practical skill is immediately useful in your role or daily responsibilities, helping you see results quickly and stay motivated.

- **Impactful:** Finally, focus on a skill that creates clear value for your employer, team, or industry. Look for something that aligns with broader goals, such as boosting revenue, improving safety, or increasing visibility. Impactful skills don't just help you—they get you noticed.

Bringing It to Life: An Example

Let's say you've decided to master presentation skills. Here's how it fits into the framework:

- ✓ **Exciting:** You love storytelling and finding creative ways to engage an audience.

- ✓ **Practical:** This skill helps you communicate ideas more effectively and solve the challenge of delivering clear, persuasive messages.

- ✓ **Impactful:** Strong presentation skills align with your goal of increasing visibility for both your team and your career.

See how this checks all three boxes? That's the kind of clarity you're aiming for. And this isn't just about growth—it's about intentional, meaningful growth that will set you apart.

13

Self-Reflection Questions

Think back to past skills you've tried to develop. Reflect on these questions:

Have you chosen skills out of weakness? Were they the right skills to focus on, or did they feel more like an obligation?

Have you ignored relevance? Did the skills align with your role or career goals, or did they end up feeling disconnected?

Have you chased trends? Were you genuinely excited about the skill, or did you lose interest quickly because it wasn't a good fit?

Reflecting on these missteps can help you avoid them as you choose your focus for the next 90 days.

Action Step

Set aside 15 minutes to brainstorm three potential skills you're considering mastering. Write them down and evaluate each one against the Exciting, Practical, and Impactful framework. Circle the skill that hits all three criteria—that's your focus for the next 90 days.

 Prompt to Share with Your Peer Network

Share your chosen skill with your accountability partner or online community. Explain why it excites you, how it's practical for your role, and the impact you expect it to create. Ask for their feedback and insights on how they've mastered similar skills. Engaging others can provide valuable perspectives and reinforce your commitment.

Closing Thought

The skill you choose to master is more than a goal—it's a catalyst for transformation. By aligning your choice with what excites you, addresses real challenges, and creates meaningful impact, you're setting the stage for growth that truly matters. This decision isn't just about the next 90 days; it's about building momentum for the career you've always envisioned.

4
MASTERING SKILLS WITH THE FASST FRAMEWORK

What if you could take control of your career and achieve incredible growth in just 90 days?

It may sound ambitious, but with the FASST Career Growth Model, it's completely within your reach.

Mastering a skill in 90 days might seem like a big challenge, but with the right roadmap, it becomes achievable and even exciting. That's where the FASST Career Growth Model comes in. Think of it as your personal guide to not just staying on track but thriving every step of the way. This model breaks your journey into five clear stages, each designed to keep you motivated, focused, and making real progress.

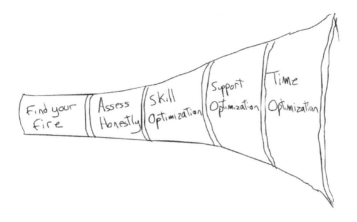

The Five Stages of the FASST Career Growth Model

The FASST Model is built around five interconnected stages that work together seamlessly. Here's how each stage contributes to your success:

1. Find Your Fire

Every journey starts with a spark—your "why."

Motivation is the energy that keeps you moving, especially when things get tough. Your "why" might be deeply personal, like wanting to support your family, or aspirational, like achieving a new career milestone. Whatever it is, identifying and connecting with your motivation gives you the drive to begin and the resilience to keep going.

2. Assess Honestly

Next, it's time to take an honest look at where you stand.

This isn't about self-criticism; it's about clarity. Assessing your current skills, strengths, and gaps helps you create a realistic plan. By knowing your starting point, you can focus your energy where it's needed most and set a baseline for measuring your progress.

3. Skill Optimization

Now, it's time to zero in on one skill—and master it.

Trying to do too much at once leads to burnout and scattered results. Instead, focus on deliberate practice and seek feedback to refine your approach. This is the stage where you'll see the magic happen: through consistent, focused effort, you'll make noticeable strides in your chosen skill.

4. Support Optimization

You don't have to do this alone.

Surround yourself with the right people—mentors, peers, and accountability partners who can offer advice, encouragement, and feedback. Leaning on a supportive community can transform your experience from a solo challenge to a shared journey of growth. It's often the difference between struggling and thriving.

5. Time Optimization

Finally, make the most of your most valuable resource: time.

Creating a realistic schedule that integrates skill-building into your daily life is key. Balance your efforts with the rest of your responsibilities, and don't forget to include time for self-care and rest. Consistency is the secret: small, regular efforts compound over time to produce remarkable results.

Why the FASST Model Works

The FASST Model works because it doesn't leave anything to chance. Each stage builds on the others, giving you a clear, connected plan for growth. Here's why it's so effective:

- ✓ **Holistic Growth:** You're not just learning a skill; you're developing the habits, mindset, and support systems that fuel long-term success.

- ✓ **Faster Results:** By focusing your energy and following a proven process, you'll see progress faster than you thought possible.

- ✓ **Sustainable Momentum:** This isn't about short bursts of effort; it's about building habits that last and creating a foundation for lifelong growth.

Think of these stages as pieces of a puzzle. Each one is essential, and together, they create a complete picture of growth, confidence, and success.

 **Self-Reflection Questions**

Which stages of the FASST Model do you feel most confident about?

Which stages might stretch you the most?

What's one small step you can take today to strengthen an area where you feel less confident?

Immediate Action Step

Take 10 minutes to outline your "draft" roadmap for the next 90 days. Don't worry about perfection—we'll refine it as we go. For now, write down one action or idea for each stage of the FASST Model:

- Find Your Fire:

- Assess Honestly:

- Skill Optimization:

- Support Optimization:

- Time Optimization:

By starting small and building momentum, you'll create a clear, actionable plan to master your chosen skill.

Prompt to Share with Your Peer Network

Share your draft roadmap with a trusted accountability partner or in an online community like The Top 10% Club. Ask for feedback and ideas to refine your plan and gain fresh perspectives. Collaboration and input from others can help you approach your goals with confidence and clarity.

Closing Thought

The FASST Career Growth Model is more than just a framework—it's a roadmap to achieving your goals with clarity, focus, and purpose. By embracing each stage, you're not only working toward mastering a skill but also building habits and systems that will serve you for a lifetime. This process isn't about perfection; it's about progress. Take the first step today, trust the model, and watch as your confidence and career growth take shape. Remember, the path to success is built one intentional step at a time.

5

COMMITTING TO YOUR GROWTH

What separates those who achieve their goals from those who don't?

It's not talent or resources—it's commitment.

You've chosen your skill and explored the FASST Career Growth Model. Now, it's time to focus on the most critical ingredient for success: committing to your growth. This commitment is the glue that holds everything together. Without it, even the best plans and strategies can fall apart. But with it? You can achieve amazing things.

I won't lie to you. Mastering a skill in 90 days won't always feel easy. There will be days when you're tired, distracted, or simply unmotivated. That's normal.

What defines your success isn't avoiding these moments but rising above them with unwavering commitment.

Celebrate Your Wins So Far

Take a moment to appreciate how far you've already come. Many people never even begin the journey of mastering a skill, but you're already several steps ahead:

✓ **You've identified a skill** that excites you, is practical, and creates impact.

✓ **You've learned how the interconnected stages** of the FASST Career Growth Model can drive accelerated results.

These are no small accomplishments. Recognizing and celebrating your wins—no matter how small—builds confidence and strengthens your motivation. Take a moment now to write down two accomplishments you're proud of since starting this journey.

The Power of Consistency

Think of consistency as the thread that stitches small actions into lasting change. The road to mastery isn't a straight line—it's filled with twists, turns, and the occasional detour. But here's the good news: you don't have to be perfect to succeed. What truly matters is showing up consistently.

Here's why consistency is so powerful:

- **Small Steps Add Up:** Even 5-10 minutes of focused effort each day can lead to significant progress over time.

- **Momentum Builds Naturally:** Each small win fuels the next, creating a snowball effect of growth.

- **Confidence Grows with Action:** The more you show up, the more capable and confident you'll feel.

Trust the process. It's not about rushing to the finish line—it's about steady, intentional progress. Every small step forward contributes to the bigger picture.

Leaning on Your Community for Support

You're not on this journey alone, and that's a powerful advantage.

Engaging with a like-minded community can transform your experience, providing the energy, accountability, and encouragement needed to keep you motivated.

Imagine sharing your successes and challenges openly, knowing that others who are on a similar path are there to cheer you on or offer a fresh perspective when you hit a roadblock. Their insights and support can be invaluable.

Seeing the progress of others can also reignite your own motivation. It's inspiring to witness how far someone else has come—and a reminder of what's possible for you, too. At the same time, celebrating their wins and offering encouragement can strengthen your connection to the group and add to the collective energy.

By leaning on your community, you're not just building your own momentum; you're contributing to a cycle of shared growth and support that lifts everyone involved.

Visualize Your Success

Close your eyes and picture yourself at the end of this journey. What does success look like for you?

- How will mastering your chosen skill boost your confidence?

- What will your peers or employer say about your growth?

- What new opportunities might this unlock for you, such as leadership roles, recognition, or exciting projects?

Reflection fuels motivation. By keeping your vision of success clear, you'll stay connected to your "why." Whenever you're feeling stuck, revisit this vision to reignite your drive.

Your Commitment Statement

To solidify your commitment, create a simple statement that you can return to whenever you need a reminder of your purpose. Here's an example:

- "I commit to showing up every day and taking consistent action to master [Skill]."

- Example: "I commit to showing up every day and taking consistent action to master presentation skills."

Self-Reflection Question

What's one area where you anticipate challenges in staying committed? How can you plan to overcome them?

Immediate Action Step

Write your commitment statement and post it somewhere important and visible in your home. This could be your bathroom mirror, refrigerator, or workspace—a place where you'll see it daily. Let this visual reminder reinforce your dedication to mastering your chosen skill.

 **Prompt to Share with Your Peer Network**

Share your commitment statement with your community or accountability network. Explain why this goal is meaningful to you and invite others to share their own commitments. By exchanging ideas and support, you'll strengthen your resolve and inspire those around you.

Closing Thought

By celebrating your wins, committing to consistency, and leaning on the power of community, you're setting yourself up for success. Growth is a journey, not a race. Every small step forward is progress. Stay focused, stay committed, and watch the incredible things you're capable of achieving unfold. You've got what it takes.

6
WHAT IS YOUR FIRE?

We all have those moments when we're unstoppable — when we're so immersed in what we're doing that time seems to fly by. That's your fire, your inner spark. But what happens when it starts to fade?

Your fire is the intrinsic motivation that drives and energizes you. It's what fuels your productivity, helps you overcome challenges, and creates a deep sense of purpose. It's the internal spark that aligns with your values, sparks enthusiasm, and gives meaning to your work. When you're connected to your fire, everything feels more purposeful and rewarding.

Why Your Fire Matters

Your fire isn't just about feeling good — it's the engine behind everything you do. It energizes you, giving you the drive to tackle challenges head-on, even when obstacles arise. This energy is contagious, fueling not only your own efforts but also inspiring those around you.

It also builds resilience. A strong sense of purpose helps you bounce back from setbacks more quickly. When you know why you're working toward a goal, it's easier to overcome roadblocks and stay the course. Finally, your fire fuels growth. When you're motivated by something meaningful, you're more likely to put in the effort required to master new skills and achieve your goals. It's the driving force behind consistent progress and long-term success.

Signs Your Fire Needs Reigniting

Sometimes, life and work can take a toll, and your fire may start to dim. Here are some signs that it might be time to reignite your fire:

- **Procrastination:** You delay tasks, even when they're important or urgent.

- **Apathy:** You feel disconnected from your work and lack enthusiasm for what you're doing.

- **Stagnation:** You're stuck in a rut, unable to make meaningful progress or feel excited about new opportunities.

- **Overwhelm:** Challenges feel insurmountable, leaving you exposed, powerless, or weighed down.

- **Irritability:** Tasks that once felt manageable now frustrate you easily.

- **Fatigue:** You feel constantly drained, even when you're not physically overworking.

- **Loss of Focus:** It's hard to concentrate, and your mind often wanders during important tasks.

- **Diminished Creativity:** Ideas that used to come easily now feel forced or nonexistent.

I've personally experienced every single one of these throughout my career. Recognizing these signs isn't a reason to feel discouraged. Instead, it's an opportunity to reflect, recalibrate, and reignite your fire. These moments are signals, not permanent states. They're invitations to step back, reassess your priorities, and reconnect with what truly matters to you.

Losing Your Fire Is a Signal, Not a Permanent State

If your fire feels like it's flickering, don't worry—you're not alone. Everyone experiences moments when their energy dips or their purpose feels unclear. Losing your fire doesn't mean you've failed. It simply means something needs to change.

Use this moment to reassess your priorities. What tasks or projects bring you the most joy and fulfillment? What aspects of your work feel misaligned? Reconnecting with your values and intrinsic motivation can help you reset. Sometimes, small shifts in perspective or action—like delegating a draining task or focusing more on what excites you—can make a world of difference.

Your fire is the foundation of your motivation and purpose. When you reconnect with it, you tap into an endless source of energy and resilience. By identifying what drives you and learning how to keep that fire alive, you set yourself up for long-term success—not just in your current goals, but in your overall career and life.

Self-Reflection Questions

Think about a time when you felt unstoppable. When have you felt your fire burn brightest in the past? What were you doing, and how did it make you feel? Reflect on moments when you were so absorbed in your work or activity that time seemed to fly by.

Now consider the opposite. What signs have you noticed when your fire starts to dim? How do those moments affect your energy and productivity? Reflecting on these experiences can help you recognize patterns and better understand what fuels your motivation.

 Immediate Action Step

Set aside 10 minutes to write down three specific actions that align with your fire. These could be tasks, projects, or habits that energize and motivate you. Keep this list somewhere visible—on your desk, your mirror, or your phone—as a daily reminder of what fuels your passion.

 **Prompt to Share with Your Peer Network**

Share one of your energizing actions with your accountability partner or online community. Explain why it connects to your fire and how it helps you stay motivated. Invite others to share their own actions for mutual inspiration and encouragement.

Closing Thought

Your fire is always there—it just needs a little spark to burn brightly again. Take the time to reconnect with it, and you'll find the energy to tackle anything that comes your way.

7
RECOGNIZING YOUR SUCCESS CLUES

Have you ever looked back on a time when you felt truly alive in your work?

Those moments hold valuable clues about what drives and energizes you. They're not just memories—they're a roadmap to understanding your fire. Every time you've felt proud, energized, or fully engaged, there's a clue about your intrinsic motivation and what fuels your growth.

By reflecting on these moments, you'll uncover patterns that point to your fire and help you take your next steps with clarity and purpose.

Reflecting on Your Success Clues

Early in my career, I worked on a project where I had to design and deliver a new training program for my team. I remember the late nights spent brainstorming creative ways to make the material engaging, and the thrill of presenting it to a room full of people. When the program was a success and colleagues expressed how it helped them, I felt an incredible sense of pride and purpose. That experience taught me that I'm most energized when I'm creating solutions and helping others grow.

Your past successes are a treasure trove of insights into what energizes and fulfills you. By taking the time to explore them, you can uncover patterns that reveal your fire and guide your next steps. Let's break this down with three key questions:

1. When Have You Felt Proud and Energized at Work?

Think about times when you set a goal, faced a challenge, and achieved something meaningful. For me, one of those moments was completing my first major client project under tight deadlines. The sense of accomplishment and recognition I received showed me how much I value overcoming challenges and delivering results.

For you, it might be landing a major project, receiving recognition from your team or employer, or contributing to meaningful business growth. These experiences highlight the types of achievements that align with your motivation.

2. When Have You Lost Track of Time?

Reflect on tasks or projects that fully absorbed your attention. I remember one afternoon spent brainstorming solutions to a tricky team conflict. Hours flew by as we worked through ideas, collaborated, and finally arrived at a strategy that worked. The flow and focus I felt in those moments told me how much I thrive in problem-solving and collaborative environments.

Maybe for you, it was writing or creating something new, solving a complex problem, or collaborating with others on an ambitious project. These moments offer powerful clues about the activities that connect deeply with your fire.

3. Why Do You Love to Do What You Do?

This open-ended question connects you with the aspects of your work that bring joy, fulfillment, or purpose. It has become my favorite question to ask anyone new I meet too, as people really get excited and light up when I ask it.

One of my favorite realizations came when I noticed how much I enjoy mentoring newer team members. Watching them succeed and grow gave me a deep sense of pride and satisfaction.

Perhaps for you, it's solving challenges that make a real difference, helping others succeed and grow, or providing for your family while building a legacy. Whatever your reasons, they form the foundation of your unique motivation.

Embracing Your Unique Motivation

The unfortunate truth is not every part of your job will light you up, and that's okay. The key is to focus on the aspects that do. Maybe it's the sense of accomplishment you feel after tackling a tough problem, the creativity you unleash when brainstorming solutions, or the joy of mentoring someone to succeed. Whatever fuels your fire, own it. It's uniquely yours, and it's the key to finding meaning and fulfillment in your work.

Your fire doesn't have to come from grand achievements—it can be fueled by personal goals, like providing for loved ones or leaving a positive impact. By embracing your unique motivation, you're better equipped to channel your energy into meaningful and fulfilling work.

Success isn't random—it leaves clues. By reflecting on your moments of pride, engagement, and joy, you can uncover the patterns that point to your intrinsic motivation.

 **Self-Reflection Question**

Think back to three moments in your career that made you feel proud and energized. What were you doing, and why did those moments stand out?

Now, think about tasks or projects where you lost track of time—what made them so engaging? Reflecting on these experiences will help you identify the activities and moments that connect with your fire.

Immediate Action Step

Choose one small step to align your work with your success clues this week. It could be something as simple as volunteering to help a colleague or starting a project you've been putting off. Small steps build big momentum.

Prompt to Share with Your Peer Network

Post your success clues with your accountability partner or community. Start by sharing what energizes you, such as: "I feel most energized when I'm mentoring others or solving challenging problems." Invite others to do the same. Sharing what drives you can spark ideas and motivation for everyone involved.

Closing Thought

Your success clues are like breadcrumbs, leading you back to your fire. Follow them, and you'll not only find what drives you—you'll ignite a career filled with purpose and energy.

8

IDENTIFING YOUR BIGGEST MOTIVATOR

Have you ever felt like your motivation was pulling you in a thousand directions? Or maybe you've struggled to figure out what truly drives you right now.

Pinpointing your biggest motivator can simplify your focus and reignite your fire.

Now that you've identified your success clues, it's time to take a closer look at what truly drives you in this moment. What's the one thing motivating you to get up and act right now?   Understanding this is a powerful way to reconnect with your fire and focus your energy where it matters most.

Maslow's Hierarchy of Needs: A Framework for Motivation

Maslow's Hierarchy of Needs provides a practical framework to uncover and align with what matters most to you right now.

What Is Maslow's Hierarchy of Needs?

Maslow's Hierarchy of Needs is like a roadmap for understanding what drives us. Picture a pyramid with five layers, each representing a different type of human need. From basic survival to self-fulfillment, these levels show how we prioritize our efforts based on where we are in life. Let's explore how this timeless framework connects to your growth:

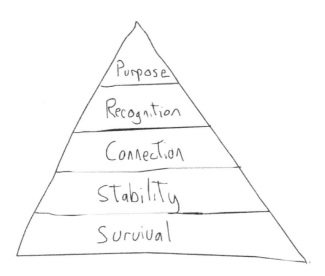

1. Physiological Needs (Survival)

These are the basics—health, rest, and financial stability. Without these foundational needs being met, it's hard to focus on higher goals.

- **Ask Yourself:** Am I getting enough rest, nourishment, and financial security to focus on growth?

- **Example:** If financial stability is your priority, you might feel most motivated by securing a steady income or improving your physical health. For instance, committing to a budget or prioritizing rest could be a game-changer.

2. Safety Needs (Stability)

Feeling secure in your job, emotional well-being, and physical safety is crucial to creating stability and confidence in your life.

- **Ask Yourself:** Do I feel secure in my job and life?

- **Example:** If job uncertainty is weighing on you, motivation might come from developing skills that make you indispensable—a smart move to create stability.

3. Love and Belonging (Connection)

Building relationships, collaborating, and feeling part of a community help satisfy our need for connection and support.

- **Ask Yourself:** Do I feel connected to supportive peers or a professional network?

- **Example:** If you're craving connection, collaborating with others or building relationships can reignite your fire by creating a sense of shared purpose.

4. Esteem (Recognition)

Feeling valued, achieving meaningful goals, and receiving recognition are powerful motivators that build confidence and drive.

- **Ask Yourself:** Do I feel recognized and proud of my work?

- **Example:** Developing a skill that leads to visible achievements—like completing a major project or earning a promotion—can fuel your confidence and motivation.

5. Self-Actualization (Purpose)

Realizing your full potential, aligning with your values, and creating impact fulfills the highest level of the hierarchy.

- **Ask Yourself:** What aligns with my passions and makes me lose track of time?

- **Example:** If you're driven by purpose, your fire might be sparked by goals like leading a team to innovation, volunteering for a cause you care about, or creating a legacy in your field.

Key Takeaways from the Hierarchy

1. **Start Where You Are:** You don't have to jump straight to self-actualization. Be honest about where you are right now and focus on what's most pressing. If financial stability is top of mind, channel your fire into creating a stronger foundation for yourself and your family.

2. **Motivation Can Change:** What drives you today might not be the same in 90 days—and that's normal! Motivation evolves with our circumstances and growth. Recognizing this helps you adapt and stay aligned with your most pressing needs.

3. **Use the Hierarchy to Reignite Your Fire:** Each level offers its own source of motivation. By aligning your efforts with your current needs, you create a pathway for meaningful progress.

Self-Reflection Questions

Think about your current situation. Are there needs you've been ignoring, like rest, connection, or recognition? Jot down how neglecting these needs might be affecting your energy, focus, or motivation.

 **Immediate Action Step**

Choose one need from the hierarchy to focus on for the next 90 days. Ask yourself: Am I motivated to eliminate discomfort or increase satisfaction in this area? Write down a specific action to get started and align with this motivator.

 **Prompt to Share with your Peer Network**

Share your biggest motivator with a trusted community or accountability partner. Here's how:

Post your current focus area and explain why it matters to you. Invite others to share their experiences or strategies for navigating similar challenges.

Read and respond to others' posts to build a sense of connection and shared motivation.

Closing Thought

Your motivator is the key to unlocking meaningful progress. Whether it's stability, connection, recognition, or purpose, aligning with your current needs allows you to take meaningful, focused action. Start where you are, and watch your fire grow as you climb higher.

9
CRAFTING YOUR FIRE STATEMENT

Your Fire Statement isn't just a sentence—it's your guiding light.

It's what keeps you focused on your purpose and pushes you forward when challenges arise.

Motivation is your spark, but action is what turns that spark into a blazing fire. To bridge the gap between your passion and your progress, let's create a Fire Statement. This simple but powerful sentence connects your intrinsic motivation to the skill you're mastering. It's your personal mantra—a reminder of why this journey matters to you, especially on tough days.

What Is a Fire Statement?

A Fire Statement is a concise and personal declaration of your "why." It ties your motivation to the skill you're working on, keeping you focused and inspired when challenges arise.

Here's the structure:

"I'm motivated to master [Skill] because [Reason]."

Examples:

- "I'm motivated to master presentation skills because I want to confidently share ideas and secure my next promotion."

- "I'm motivated to master leadership skills because I want to inspire my team and create a positive workplace culture."

Imagine this: You're working late, feeling drained, and questioning why you started this journey. Then you glance at your Fire Statement: "I'm motivated to master public speaking because I want to inspire and lead my team." Suddenly, you remember your purpose, and that spark reignites.

Think of your Fire Statement as your North Star — the thing that keeps you moving forward no matter what.

How to Create Your Fire Statement

Let's break this down into three easy steps:

Step 1: Identify Your Skill

What skill have you committed to mastering in the next 90 days? If you're unsure or want to refine your choice, revisit your reflections from earlier chapters. Be specific about what you want to focus on. For example, if your skill is "data analysis," clarify whether you're focusing on improving efficiency, mastering specific tools, or drawing actionable insights.

Step 2: Reflect on Your Fire

Why does this skill matter to you? What drives you? Here are a few reasons to consider:

- ✓ Achieving job security.
- ✓ Building confidence.
- ✓ Providing for your family.
- ✓ Advancing your career.

✓ Making a meaningful impact.

Reflect on what excites you about this skill. Is it the ability to solve problems, gain recognition, or achieve personal growth? Take a moment to think deeply about what resonates most with you.

Step 3: Write Your Statement

Combine your skill and your motivation into one clear sentence. Make it personal, authentic, and inspiring.

Examples:

- "I'm motivated to master coding because I want to build innovative solutions that improve people's lives."

- "I'm motivated to master communication skills because I want to connect deeply with my clients and grow my business."

Refining Your Fire Statement

Take a moment to read your Fire Statement out loud. Does it feel true and powerful to you? If not, tweak it until it resonates.

Ask Yourself:

- Does this statement inspire me to keep going when things get hard?

- Does it feel specific and personal?

For example:

- If "job security" feels too vague, try refining it to "ensuring financial stability for my family."

43

- If "personal growth" feels too broad, narrow it down to "increasing my confidence in public speaking."

A great Fire Statement should evoke a strong emotional connection. Ask yourself: Does this make me feel proud? Does it remind me of the bigger picture? Your Fire Statement is more than just words—it's your anchor, your compass, your rallying cry. When obstacles arise, it reminds you of your deeper purpose and keeps you moving forward.

Self-Reflection Question

What drives you to master this skill? Reflect on the deeper purpose behind your motivation and consider how it aligns with your goals and values.

Immediate Action Step

Take 10 minutes to craft your Fire Statement. Write it down and place it somewhere visible, like your workspace or journal. Commit to revisiting it daily to keep your motivation front and center.

Prompt to Share with your Peer Network

Amplify the power of your Fire Statement by sharing it with a supportive community. Here's how:

Share your Fire Statement and explain why it matters to you. Comment on others' posts, offer encouragement, and celebrate their commitments.

By sharing, you're not just inspiring yourself—you're lifting others up, too.

Closing Thought

Your Fire Statement is a declaration of your purpose and potential. It's a reminder of why you started and a source of strength when the journey gets tough. Craft it with care, revisit it often, and let it fuel your journey toward mastery and success. Start where you are and let your Fire Statement guide you forward.

10
ASSESSING YOUR SKILL LEVEL

Imagine setting out on a road trip without knowing where you're starting from.

It would be impossible to chart your route! The same applies to personal growth—you can't reach your destination without first understanding your current position. Assessing your skill level honestly isn't about judgment or perfection; it's about clarity. When you understand your strengths and areas for growth, you can focus your efforts on where they'll make the biggest impact.

What Is an Honest Assessment?

Think of an honest assessment as your GPS for growth. It helps you figure out exactly where you are so you can decide where to go next. It's not about passing or failing—it's about finding clarity.

Why It Matters:

- **Clarity Beats Guesswork:** You'll know what to focus on instead of wasting time on guesswork.

- **Growth Starts Here:** Identifying gaps gives you the roadmap to improvement.

- **No Judgment, Just Progress:** This isn't about being perfect; it's about knowing yourself.

The Dunning-Kruger Effect: Confidence vs. Competence

Have you ever felt super confident starting something new, only to realize later how much you didn't know? That's the Dunning-Kruger Effect in action. This handy framework explains the rollercoaster of confidence and competence we all experience when learning something new.

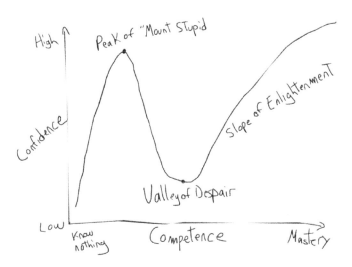

Here's the Journey:

- **Peak of Mount Stupid:** At the start, you might feel like you've got it all figured out. Confidence is sky-high, but competence is low.

- **Valley of Despair:** Then reality kicks in. You realize how much there is to learn, and your confidence takes a nosedive.

- **Slope of Enlightenment:** With consistent effort, your confidence and competence start to align. This is where steady progress happens.

When I first started learning how to present to an audience, I felt unstoppable after watching a few videos of great presenters. I thought I had it all figured out. Then I stood in front of crowd of business owners in Northern Michigan. It became clear VERY quickly how little I knew about presenting—that's the Valley of Despair. I had my back turned to the audience. I made a bunch of mistakes. With time and effort, I climbed the Slope of Enlightenment, building both confidence and competence.

Knowing where you are on this curve helps you navigate the ups and downs of learning. It's a reminder that feeling stuck or overwhelmed is part of the process—and it's temporary.

Steps to Conduct an Honest Assessment

1. Reflect on Your Current Skill Level

Ask yourself: Where do I excel in this skill? Where do I struggle? Be as specific as possible. Consider your recent performance:

- Have you received feedback from others?

- Are there specific tasks where you feel most confident or unsure?

For example, if you're working on public speaking, you might excel at organizing your thoughts but struggle with delivering confidently.

2. Use the Dunning-Kruger Curve

Are you overestimating your abilities? Be honest with yourself. Think about past projects:

- Did your initial confidence align with your actual results?

- Were there areas where you overestimated your abilities?

Acknowledge gaps as opportunities for growth and embrace the Valley of Despair—it's where the magic of learning happens.

3. Prepare for Growth

Confidence might dip as you uncover challenges, and that's okay. Focus on your strengths while addressing your gaps. Celebrate every small win as you move forward. Growth is a journey, not a destination, and every step forward matters.

Honest Self-Assessment: A Gift of Clarity

Honest self-assessment isn't about tearing yourself down—it's about giving yourself the gift of clarity. By understanding your strengths, identifying your gaps, and recognizing where you are on the Dunning-Kruger curve, you create a roadmap for growth. It's the first step toward meaningful, measurable progress.

Self-Reflection Question

Think back to a time when you overestimated or underestimated your skills. What did you learn from that experience, and how did it shape your approach to growth?

Immediate Action Step

Take 10 minutes to conduct your own honest assessment. Write down:

- Three specific strengths you bring to this skill
- Three areas where you struggle or feel unsure.

As you identify your strengths, think about how they've helped you succeed in the past. For your struggles, consider whether they've held you back or created learning opportunities.

Prompt to Share with your Peer Network

Reflection becomes even more powerful when you share it with others.

Share your reflections with a community of like-minded learners. Normalize the ups and downs of learning and inspire others. Read others' stories, celebrate their wins, and exchange insights. Growth is better when it's shared.

Closing Thought

Growth isn't about perfection—it's about progress. By embracing where you are today, you set the stage for where you want to go. Remember, every step forward counts, no matter how small. Take the time to assess honestly and create a foundation for meaningful progress.

11
MAPPING YOUR SKILL GROWTH

Imagine having a clear plan that not only defines success but also shows you exactly how to get there.

That's what skill mapping offers—an actionable roadmap to make your growth intentional and measurable. By breaking your chosen skill into competencies and measurable indicators, you'll create a clear path to mastery over the next 90 days.

Let's dive in and make your growth journey as targeted and impactful as possible.

What Are Competencies and Performance Indicators?

Think of competencies as the building blocks of your skill. They're the core components that define what success looks like. For example, in public speaking, a competency might be **"Audience Engagement."**

Performance indicators, on the other hand, are like signposts—they show you exactly how to measure your progress within each competency. For "Audience Engagement," a performance indicator could be: **"Use interactive techniques like polls or storytelling to**

maintain audience attention."

Think of competencies as the ingredients of a recipe and performance indicators as the step-by-step instructions. Together, they ensure you're building your skill with precision and clarity. Breaking your skill into these parts gives you focus. Instead of feeling overwhelmed, you'll know exactly what to work on.

Leveraging AI for Skill Mapping

Creating a competency map might sound daunting, but here's the good news: AI tools like ChatGPT can help you do it quickly and effectively. With just a few prompts, you can generate a tailored roadmap for your skill.

How AI Helps:

- **Saves Time:** AI can quickly outline competencies and indicators, saving you hours of brainstorming.

- **Provides Clarity:** It ensures you have a complete and structured view of your skill.

- **Customizes for You:** The output is tailored to your specific skill and goals.

Prompt Example:

Try this to get started: *"I want to develop my skill of [Skill] in the next 90 days. What are the high-impact competencies and measurable performance indicators from beginner to mastery?"*

When I first tried using AI for skill mapping, I wasn't sure what to expect. But within minutes, I had a detailed roadmap for improving my presentation skills, complete with actionable indicators. It saved me hours of brainstorming and gave me a clear focus.

It's like having a coach who's ready to create a custom plan just for you.

Using the Output to Self-Assess

Once you have your competency map, it's time to evaluate where you are right now. Don't worry—this isn't about being perfect. It's about getting a clear picture of where to focus your energy.

Steps to Self-Assess:

1. **Rate Yourself:** For each competency and performance indicator, rate yourself on a scale from 1 to 10. Be honest. This is your starting point.

2. **Identify Gaps:** Look for areas where your scores are lowest. These gaps are your biggest opportunities for growth.

Example Assessment:

Competency: Content Design and Structure

- **Beginner:** "Create a basic outline for a 5-10 minute presentation." (9/10)

- **Intermediate:** "Use storytelling and examples to make content engaging." (5/10)

- **Mastery:** "Structure presentations to convey complex ideas effectively." (3/10)

For instance, I rated myself a 5/10 on storytelling because while I can come up with examples, I struggle to weave them into a cohesive narrative during presentations. In this example, the biggest growth opportunity is moving from intermediate to mastery.

Mapping Your Growth Path

Mapping out competencies and performance indicators isn't just a planning exercise—it's a way to turn vague goals into actionable steps. This is what sets people in the top 10% of their field apart from everyone else. Most people do not take the time or effort to do this, so they remain stagnant and do not grow. By defining success and measuring progress, you'll focus on the areas that truly matter. This process ensures that your efforts are meaningful and sets you up for real, measurable growth.

Self-Reflection Question

What competency or performance indicator excites you the most, and why? Reflect on how focusing on it could create meaningful progress in your growth journey.

Immediate Action Steps

Now it's time to prioritize. Choose one competency to focus on for the next 90 days. This focus ensures your efforts are intentional and impactful.

1. **Generate Your Map:** Use AI to create a detailed list of competencies and indicators.

2. **Rate Yourself:** Evaluate your current proficiency honestly.

3. **Pick Your Focus:** Select the area with the highest potential for growth.

Prompt to Share with Your Peer Network

Growth is even more powerful when it's shared. Post your chosen competency and goals in a supportive community. Here's how:

Let others know what you're working on and why it matters. Celebrate their goals and exchange ideas for growth.

Closing Thought

Skill mapping isn't just about identifying gaps; it's about celebrating where you are and building a path to where you want to be. Each step forward, no matter how small, is progress. Use your competency map as your guide and take each step with intention. Remember, progress happens one focused effort at a time—and every effort brings you closer to mastery.

12
EMBRACING FEEDBACK FOR GROWTH

Have you ever been blindsided by feedback you didn't expect? Maybe it stung, or maybe it sparked a breakthrough.

Feedback, when embraced, can be one of the most powerful tools for growth.

You've done an incredible job assessing your skills so far, but here's the truth: we all have blind spots. That's where feedback comes in. Imagine having someone point out hidden opportunities for growth or confirm that you're on the right track. Feedback from others adds a layer of depth and clarity that self-assessment alone can't provide.

If I'm being honest with myself, feedback used to be something I dreaded. I remember one moment early in my career when a colleague pointed out that my presentations were clear but lacked energy. At first, I was defensive, thinking, "Well, at least they're clear!" But when I reflected on it, I realized they were right. That feedback led me to focus on engaging delivery techniques, which transformed how I present today. Over time, I realized that feedback wasn't criticism—it was a tool for growth. Once I understood that feedback could help me improve and have a bigger impact, I started leaning into it more. Embracing feedback transformed my approach to skill development and made me a better leader and professional.

Let's dive into how feedback can take your skill development to the next level.

Why Feedback Matters

Self-assessment is a powerful starting point, but feedback adds fresh perspectives that help you see the full picture. Here's why it's essential:

- **Uncover Blind Spots:** Others can highlight areas for improvement that you might not notice, like filler words in presentations or unclear messaging. Feedback is like having a second set of eyes on a painting you've been staring at for hours. They'll notice the details you've missed and suggest ways to make your work even better.

- **Validate Strengths:** Hearing what you're doing well builds confidence and helps you double down on your strengths.

- **Offer New Perspectives:** External viewpoints can spark new ideas or help you see your skill from a different angle.

Feedback is like a mirror—it reflects both your potential and your growth opportunities.

The Who, What, and How of Feedback

One of the biggest mistakes I made around feedback was not asking the right people. Let's jump into the **Who**, the **What**, and the **How** of Feedback to ensure you're making the most of it.

Who to Ask for Feedback

The quality of your feedback depends on who you ask. A best practice is to choose people who:

- **Know Your Work:** They've seen you in action and understand your skill.

- **Understand the Skill:** They have enough expertise to provide specific, actionable advice.

- **Care About Your Growth:** They genuinely want to see you succeed and will give constructive, supportive feedback.

Avoid asking someone who doesn't understand the skill you're working on, as their feedback might be generic or uninformed. Similarly, steer clear of overly critical individuals who may undermine your confidence rather than build it.

Example: A mentor who's familiar with your presentations and has expertise in public speaking is an ideal choice to provide feedback on audience engagement.

What to Ask

Good feedback starts with good questions. Focus on targeted, manageable prompts to get the insights you need:

This is My Favorite Two-Question Strategy:

1. What's one thing I do well with [Skill]?
2. What's one area where I could improve?

Competency-Specific Questions: Use the performance indicators you created earlier to guide the conversation.

- "How effectively do I use techniques like storytelling or polls to connect with my audience?"

Focused questions ensure that the feedback is relevant and valuable. General questions will typically get general answers.

How to Receive Feedback

Feedback is a gift, but how you receive it can make all the difference. Here's how to get the most out of it:

- **Listen Openly:** Stay curious and avoid interrupting, defending, or dismissing feedback. If you feel defensive, take a deep breath and remind yourself that feedback is about the work, not about you as a person. It's okay to take a moment to process before responding.

- **Ask for Clarity:** If something isn't clear, ask for specifics. For example: "Can you give me an example of where my messaging felt unclear?"

- **Show Gratitude:** Thank the person for their time and insights. Gratitude encourages more feedback in the future.

Once you've gathered feedback, it's time to put it to work. Combine it with your self-assessment to refine your understanding of your strengths and gaps.

Self-Reflection Question

Think about the last piece of feedback you received. How did you respond to it, and what did you learn from the experience?

Immediate Action Step

Take 15 minutes to gather feedback from one trusted person this week. Ask them the two questions above and one competency-specific question. Consider how the feedback aligns with your self-assessment. Reflect on their insights and write down one action you'll take based on their feedback.

Prompt to Share with Your Peer Network

Sharing what you've learned not only reinforces your growth but also inspires others. Here's how to do it:

Share the feedback you received and how it's shaping your next steps. Comment on their posts, exchange tips, and celebrate wins together.

Closing Thought

Feedback isn't just about finding areas to improve—it's about building confidence, gaining fresh perspectives, and accelerating your journey toward mastery. Growth thrives on feedback. The more you embrace it, the more you unlock your potential. Let each piece of feedback be a stepping stone toward the version of yourself you aspire to be.

13
TURNING INSIGHT INTO ACTION

You've reflected, gathered feedback, and identified your areas for growth. Now it's time for the most exciting part: action.

This is where your vision turns into tangible results. This chapter is your bridge between dreaming and doing—we're turning your vision of growth into a clear, step-by-step roadmap that gets real results.

Let's roll up our sleeves and make it happen!

Identifying Your Key Competency

First things first: let's narrow your focus. Growth happens when you channel your energy into the areas that matter most, so we're going to choose one key competency to work on.

Look back at your self-assessment and feedback. Pick the competency that feels the most impactful or relevant right now.

When I first worked on public speaking, I realized my presentations lacked audience engagement. By focusing on just that one competency for 90 days, I transformed not just my delivery but the way my audience responded.

Defining Performance Indicators and Goals

Now that you've chosen your focus, it's time to get specific about what success looks like. Performance indicators break down your competency into measurable milestones, while 90-day goals give you a clear target to aim for.

Performance indicators are specific, trackable outcomes that show progress within your chosen competency. They eliminate guesswork and keep you focused. More importantly, they let you see how far you've come, which helps build momentum and creates a snowball effect.

For **"Audience Engagement,"** a performance indicator could be:

- **Engaging Questions:** Two open-ended questions per presentation with a 30% audience response rate.

Using AI to Define Indicators

AI tools like ChatGPT can help you create meaningful performance indicators quickly. Here's a prompt to get started:

"Help me identify three measurable performance indicators for [Skill], with trackable metrics and 90-day targets."

Example Results for "Audience Engagement":

1. **Engaging Questions:** Two open-ended questions per presentation with a 30% audience response rate. Open-ended questions not only increase engagement but also help you gauge audience understanding in real-time.

2. **Memorable Storytelling:** One compelling story per session, with 50% of follow-up responses referencing the story. Stories make your message stick, leaving a lasting impression.

3. **Interactive Activities:** One poll or group discussion per session, with 50% audience participation. Interaction ensures that your audience stays active and connected to your content.

Why This Process Matters

This level of planning and precision is what sets high performers apart. Most people never take the time to define clear performance indicators or set measurable goals. By doing this, you're already setting yourself apart as someone committed to real, measurable growth.

While most people stay stuck in vague goals and unstructured efforts, you're building a clear, actionable plan for measurable growth. By focusing on what matters and tracking your progress, you'll achieve more in 90 days than many do in a year.

Self-Reflection Question

What is one competency that, if improved, would have the biggest impact on your growth right now? Why does it matter?

Immediate Action Steps

1. **Identify Your Key Competency:** Based on your self-assessment and feedback, choose one to focus on.

2. **Generate Measurable Performance Indicators:** Use AI or

brainstorming to create three specific indicators.

3. **Define 90-Day Goals:** Write down clear targets for each indicator.

Prompt to Share with Your Peer Network

Share your chosen competency and performance indicators with your community. Here's how:

Share the competency you're working on and why it's important to you. Include your 90-day performance indicators and what success looks like.

Invite feedback, tips, or resources from others who've worked on similar goals.

Closing Thought

This is your moment to step forward with clarity and purpose. By setting clear goals and breaking them into measurable steps, you're creating a roadmap to success. This intentional approach will not only help you stay focused but also ensure that your efforts lead to meaningful, lasting results. Let's get started—your next level of growth is waiting!

14
PRACTICING SMARTER: THE GAME-CHANGING STRATEGIES FOR MASTERY

Mastering a skill doesn't have to feel like an endless uphill climb.

With the right strategies, you can fast-track your growth, stay motivated, and even enjoy the journey. Skill mastery isn't about grinding away endlessly; it's about working smarter, not harder.

In this chapter, we're going to explore three proven methods that make practicing your skill feel purposeful: **focused practice**, **spaced repetition**, and **active learning**. These aren't just fancy techniques— they're game-changers that will help you stay on track and make real progress.

Let's dive in.

1. Focused Practice

Trying to improve everything all at once can feel overwhelming and unproductive. That's where focused practice comes in. It helps you zoom in on the specific areas of your skill that need the most attention—one step at a time. Focused practice is about deliberate effort on targeted areas, making your growth intentional and impactful.

Most people don't practice with focus, and that's a big reason why progress stalls. Instead of isolating the skills they need to improve, they fall into patterns of mindless repetition. For example, someone trying to improve their public speaking might repeatedly deliver an entire speech without addressing their weak points, like a monotone voice or poor transitions. This approach might feel productive, but it's often just reinforcing bad habits.

How It Works:

- **Isolate the Problem:** Identify a specific challenge within your competency. For example, if you struggle with audience engagement, isolate whether it's due to weak storytelling, lack of eye contact, or ineffective Q&A handling.

- **Create a Practice Plan:** Dedicate short, focused sessions to this specific area. For instance, spend 10 minutes crafting a single compelling story for your presentation, then practice delivering it with varied intonations.

- **Track Progress:** Measure how your improvements impact your overall competency. Use feedback or video recordings to assess growth.

Think of an athlete perfecting a free throw. Instead of playing full games, they focus on just that one shot, repeating and refining until it's second nature. Focused practice concentrates your efforts and lets you make meaningful changes, one detail at a time. By addressing specific areas rather than attempting everything at once, you'll make measurable progress and avoid the frustration of feeling stuck.

2. Spaced Repetition

You know that feeling when you learn something new, and a week later it feels like it vanished from your brain? Spaced repetition is the antidote to that. It's all about revisiting what you've learned at regular intervals, so it actually sticks for good.

Most people approach learning with a one-and-done mindset. They cram information or practice a skill in one long session, expecting it to stick. But the human brain doesn't work that way. Without reinforcement, your brain starts to forget what it learned, a phenomenon called the "Forgetting Curve."

How It Works:

- **Practice at Increasing Intervals:** Day 1, Day 3, Day 7, Day 14, and so on. Revisiting material at intervals helps transfer knowledge from short-term to long-term memory.

- **Build on Each Session:** Each practice session requires you to retrieve what you've learned, strengthening neural pathways and making the skill easier to access in the future.

Example: Engaging the Audience

- **Day 1:** Practice crafting and delivering two open-ended questions.
- **Day 3:** Test those questions in a small meeting and note audience reactions.
- **Day 7:** Refine your delivery based on feedback and practice again.
- **Day 14:** Use the questions in a larger presentation and evaluate your progress.

Spaced repetition is like watering a plant. Each session is a small but vital step that helps your skill grow and thrive. Musicians rehearse songs over weeks, not hours, to perfect their performance. With each practice, your confidence and competence deepen, ensuring that your learning becomes second nature.

3. Active Learning

The best way to grow is by doing. Active learning means jumping in, testing your skills in real-world situations, and learning from experience. It's fast, it's practical, and it works—but surprisingly, it's often underutilized.

Most people stay stuck in preparation mode. They spend hours reading about a skill or attending workshops but hesitate to put their knowledge into action. While theory is useful, it only takes you so far.

Active learning helps you close the gap between knowing and doing, forcing you to face real-world challenges and adapt. This builds confidence, adaptability, and a deep understanding of your skill.

How It Works:

- **Find Low-Stakes Opportunities:** Start small. Look for settings where you can test your skills without overwhelming pressure, such as team meetings, practice groups, or one-on-one settings.

- **Focus on One Element at a Time:** If you're improving your presentation skills, focus on storytelling in one session and pacing in the next.

- **Reflect and Adapt:** After each attempt, ask yourself or others what went well and what could be improved. Use this feedback to make targeted adjustments.

If you're learning coding, active learning might mean building a small, real-world app instead of just following tutorials. Active learning transforms theory into action and builds your confidence every step of the way. It's not about being perfect from the start—it's about growing through experience and refining your approach with each iteration.

Takeaways

These three strategies are your power tools for skill mastery:

✓ **Focused Practice:** Zero in on specific areas for big gains by breaking down your goals into manageable pieces.

✓ **Spaced Repetition:** Strengthen your learning over time by revisiting and refining what you've learned.

✓ **Active Learning:** Dive in, get hands-on, and grow through real-world experience.

When you use these strategies together, you'll build momentum that keeps you moving forward. Focused practice hones your weak spots, spaced repetition locks in your learning, and active learning ensures real-world application. Together, they form a powerhouse approach to mastery.

Self-Reflection Question

Which of these strategies—focused practice, spaced repetition, or active learning—do you currently use the least? How could you start incorporating it into your practice routine?

Immediate Action Step

Choose one of the three strategies to focus on this week. Write down a specific plan for how you will implement it. For example:

• **Focused Practice:** Spend 10 minutes each day addressing a specific weak point in your skill.

- **Spaced Repetition:** Schedule practice sessions at increasing intervals.

- **Active Learning:** Identify one real-world opportunity to test your skills and commit to doing it.

Prompt to Share with Your Peer Network

Share your strategy choice and plan with your community. Here's how:

Share which strategy you're focusing on and why it's important to you. Describe your specific plan for implementation.

Ask for tips or encouragement from others who have used similar strategies.

Closing Thought

Mastery isn't just about effort—it's about strategy. By practicing smarter, not harder, you're setting yourself up for exponential growth. Embrace the process, and you'll be amazed at the progress you make in your journey toward mastery.

15
SELECTING THE RIGHT RESOURCES: TOOLS FOR TARGETED GROWTH

Have you ever felt overwhelmed by the sheer number of resources out there?

It's easy to get lost in a sea of materials that promise results but leave you spinning your wheels. The right tools can make all the difference in your growth journey.

Not every book, course, or video is worth your time—and that's okay. The secret to rapid growth is selecting resources that are laser-focused on your needs.

Why Picking the Right Resources is a Game-Changer

Choosing the right resources is like having a map that guides you straight to your destination. Instead of wasting time wading through irrelevant or generic materials, you can focus on tools that are designed specifically for your needs.

This approach not only saves time but ensures that every moment spent learning moves you closer to your goals. The right resources give you clarity, helping you skip the fluff and focus on actionable insights that you can apply immediately.

Beyond efficiency, the right resources also keep you from feeling overwhelmed. By prioritizing quality over quantity, learning becomes a manageable and rewarding process. When your tools align with your goals, each piece of knowledge becomes a stepping stone, propelling you forward with purpose and confidence.

The Three Critical Criteria for Resource Selection

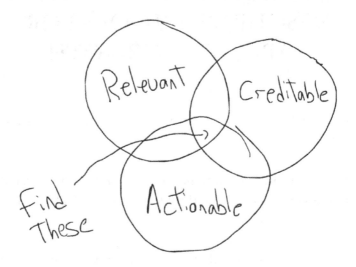

Choosing the right resources is a critical step in mastering any skill, but the process can feel overwhelming without a clear approach. Here, we'll break down how to apply the suggested criteria— Relevance, Credibility, and Actionability—to ensure the resources you choose align with your unique goals and context.

1. Relevance: Finding What Fits Your Goals

The most effective resources are those tailored to your specific skill and current level of expertise. To determine relevance, start by asking:

- **What skill am I focusing on?** Narrow down your objective.

For example, if you're improving public speaking, decide whether you need help with storytelling, delivery, or audience engagement.

- **What's my current proficiency level?** Look for resources designed for beginners, intermediates, or advanced learners, depending on where you are.

- **Does this resource address my specific challenge?** If your goal is to engage audiences better, a tutorial on crafting open-ended questions will be more relevant than a general public speaking book.

Example: If you're a manager aiming to improve team communication, choose resources like case studies or courses focused on leadership communication techniques instead of generic management books.

2. Credibility: Ensuring You Learn from the Best

Not all resources are created equal. To assess credibility:

- **Who is the author or creator?** Look for experts with proven experience or credentials in your field.

- **What's the reputation of the source?** Check reviews, testimonials, or recommendations from trusted peers.

- **Are there success stories or data to back up their claims?** Credible resources often showcase case studies or user feedback that demonstrate effectiveness.

Example: If you're learning data analysis, a course taught by an industry professional with years of experience and positive reviews will likely be more credible than a free, unverified blog post.

3. Actionability: Prioritizing Practical Steps

The best resources not only teach concepts but also provide clear, actionable steps you can implement immediately. When evaluating a resource, ask:

- **Does this include exercises, templates, or examples?** These features help you apply what you learn.

- **Can I see immediate results?** Look for tools that encourage you to practice as you learn, such as interactive quizzes or hands-on projects.

- **Does it align with my schedule?** Practicality includes finding resources that fit within your time constraints.

Example: If your goal is to master Excel, choose a course with downloadable spreadsheets and practice problems over a video lecture series that doesn't encourage hands-on learning.

Applying the Criteria in Your Context

To make this process actionable, create a quick checklist based on the criteria:

- ✓ **Relevance:** Does this resource address my skill focus and level?

- ✓ **Credibility:** Is the creator an expert, and is there evidence of success?

- ✓ **Actionability:** Will this resource help me practice and see results quickly?

By applying this checklist, you'll filter out irrelevant, low-quality, or overly theoretical resources, ensuring that each tool you select aligns with your unique needs and goals.

Pro Tip: Leverage AI for Personalized Recommendations

Tools like ChatGPT can help you find tailored resources quickly. Use precise prompts to save time and gain clarity.

Example Prompt: "What are the best resources for improving storytelling in public speaking for an intermediate-level speaker? Focus on relevance, credibility, and actionability."

This approach ensures that you're not only finding resources but also aligning them with your context and objectives. By focusing on these criteria, you'll streamline your learning journey and make measurable progress toward mastering your skill.

Self-Reflection Question

What was your biggest challenge when selecting resources in the past? Have you ever spent time on a resource that didn't align with your goals, and what did you learn from that experience?

Immediate Action Step

Take 15 minutes to build your resource list. Look for one resource that meets each of the three criteria: relevance, credibility, and actionability. Use AI, community recommendations, or trusted sources to expand your search.

Prompt to Share with You Peer Network

Collaborating with a community not only multiplies your learning opportunities but also connects you with materials you might not find on your own. The best insights often come from people walking the same path as you.

Post about a resource you've discovered and explain how it aligns with your goals. Invite others to share resources they've found valuable for similar goals.

Discuss what worked (or didn't) to refine your choices and save time for everyone.

Closing Thought

Selecting the right resources isn't just about finding tools—it's about empowering yourself with knowledge that aligns with your unique goals. By focusing on relevance, credibility, and actionability, you're ensuring that every moment you invest in learning drives meaningful progress. The journey to mastery is made smoother when you have the right guidance. Start curating your resource list today and watch as your efforts transform into impactful growth.

16
LEVERAGING TECHNOLOGY FOR SKILL GROWTH

Imagine having access to tools that save you hours of time, tailor your learning to your exact needs, and make practice more enjoyable than ever before.

The reality is most people aren't tapping into the full potential of technology. Instead, they rely on outdated methods, generic resources, or tools that distract more than they help. This leads to slower progress and unnecessary frustration.

We're at a point where modern tools like AI, online courses, and interactive platforms are impossible to ignore. This chapter will show you how to unlock the power of technology to supercharge your skill-building journey. Let's dive in.

Why Technology Matters for Skill Development

Efficiency:

Technology eliminates unnecessary steps and lets you focus on what truly drives progress. Tools like AI assistants can generate tailored insights or create practice scenarios in seconds, saving you hours of effort. Imagine having AI create a practice scenario for you instantly instead of spending hours preparing on your own.

Engagement:

Interactive platforms and gamified apps transform learning into an enjoyable experience. Instead of dreading practice, you'll find yourself motivated to return to your tools regularly, keeping your momentum strong.

Customization:

Modern tools adapt learning to your unique goals. For instance, public speaking simulators can focus specifically on improving audience engagement, while coding platforms can align with your current project needs.

Feedback at Your Fingertips:

Immediate, actionable feedback from AI tools like Grammarly or technical training simulators helps you course-correct in real time. This prevents mistakes from becoming habits and accelerates your mastery.

Scalability:

Technology grows with you. As you progress, you can explore advanced tools or dive deeper into specialized platforms, ensuring your resources always match your level of expertise.

When used effectively, technology makes your growth journey smoother, more engaging, and laser-focused on results.

Top Tools and Platforms to Enhance Learning

1. Online Courses:

Platforms like LinkedIn Learning, Udemy, and specialized resources such as the Top 10% Club offer expert-led, step-by-step guides.

Example: If your goal is mastering time management, check out "Time Mastery for Leaders" on LinkedIn Learning. This top-rated course breaks down practical strategies in under two hours. These courses are ideal for structured, comprehensive learning. When choosing a course, ensure it aligns with your specific competency and goals.

2. AI Assistants:

Tools like ChatGPT and Google Bard provide:

- Tailored insights for your skill.
- Simulated scenarios for practice.
- Idea generation to deepen your understanding.

Example: If you're mastering public speaking, you can ask ChatGPT to simulate an audience Q&A session or generate feedback on your messaging. I used ChatGPT to draft a mock audience Q&A for a presentation—it highlighted gaps in my preparation I hadn't noticed.

3. Interactive Tutorials:

Apps like Khan Academy, Codecademy, and Duolingo combine gamification with learning for a more engaging experience. These are particularly effective for breaking complex concepts into manageable lessons and keeping you motivated.

4. Knowledge Organizers:

Tools like Google Drive or Notion allow you to store, organize, and access curated knowledge quickly. They're perfect for keeping all your resources in one place, making it easier to revisit and review materials.

Using Technology to Practice Effectively

Learning is just the first step. Practice solidifies your knowledge and builds confidence. Here's how tech can make practice more effective:

1. Simulations and Practice Platforms:

Virtual environments replicate real-world scenarios for repeated practice. For example:

- **Public Speaking Simulators:** Refine delivery and tone with AI-driven feedback.

- **Technical Training Platforms:** Solve hands-on problems in coding, engineering, or project management.

These platforms give you a safe space to experiment and improve. Toastmasters or LeetCode, for example, are industry-specific tools that can elevate your skills.

2. AI Feedback Tools:

Tools like Grammarly and AI language tutors provide immediate, actionable feedback. They help you identify specific areas for improvement, making each practice session more impactful.

3. Skill-Specific Practice Apps:

Apps tailored to specific skills—like Duolingo for language learning, Canva for design, or Yousician for music practice—gamify the process, making practice fun and encouraging consistency. These apps turn routine practice into a rewarding experience.

 ### Self-Reflection Question

How have you been using technology in your skill-building journey so far? Are there any tools or methods you've overlooked that could help you achieve better results?

Immediate Action Steps

Now it's your turn to put these tools into action. Reflect on your chosen skill and competency. What do you need most? Learning, practice, or both?

Take 15 minutes to research and identify relevant technology resources for structured learning practice scenarios.

Prompt to Share with Your Peer Network

Share how you're using technology to enhance your learning or practice in a supportive community.

Share one tool you've chosen for learning and one for practice. Explain why they align with your goals. Invite others to suggest their favorite tech tools or share experiences with similar goals.

Comment on posts, exchange insights, and celebrate progress together.

Closing Thought

By embracing the power of technology, you're not just learning—you're transforming the way you grow. These tools are here to amplify your efforts, accelerate your progress, and make mastery achievable. Start exploring today, and watch how technology turns obstacles into stepping stones on your journey to success.

17
ADJUSTING YOUR STRATEGIES

Have you ever felt like you're putting in the work but not seeing the results you want?

It's not about working harder—it's about working smarter by adjusting your strategies along the way. Progress isn't just about moving forward—it's about learning, adapting, and growing as you go.

Adjusting your strategies ensures that you stay aligned with your goals, overcome roadblocks, and make the most of your efforts.

Most of us fall into the trap of sticking with the same strategies, even when they're not delivering the results we want. It's easy to get comfortable or assume that more effort will eventually pay off. I used to think the same way—until I realized that refining my approach was the key to unlocking real growth. Failing to adjust isn't a failure; it's an opportunity to pivot and improve.

In this chapter, we're going to explore the "Start, Stop, Continue" method—a simple and effective way to measure progress and refine your strategies. Let's turn your reflections into powerful adjustments that keep you on the path to success.

Why Do We Hesitate to Adjust Strategies?

1. **Fear of Change:** Trying something new can feel risky or uncomfortable, especially when you're already invested in your current methods. It's like sticking to a familiar route in traffic even when there's a faster one—change feels risky, even if it's logical.

2. **Lack of Awareness:** Sometimes, we don't even realize what's not working until we take a step back to evaluate. Being so deep in the work often blinds us to signs that it's time to switch gears.

3. **Effort Over Strategy:** We often equate grinding harder with success, forgetting that smarter adjustments can yield faster results. If the ladder is against the wrong wall, climbing faster won't help.

By reflecting on what's working and making intentional tweaks, you can break through plateaus and unlock new levels of growth. Adjusting your strategies isn't a sign of failure; it's a sign of growth.

Why It Works:

- **Stay Aligned:** Make sure your efforts are always pointing toward your goals.

- **Break Through Barriers:** Identify and tackle anything that's slowing you down.

- **Maximize Results:** Focus your time and energy on what truly works.

Think of adjustments as course corrections. They're what keep you moving forward, even when the path gets a little bumpy.

The Start, Stop, Continue Method

I didn't come up with this method, but in my experience, it's one of the simplest yet most powerful techniques to figure out what's working, what's not, and what new ideas you can try.

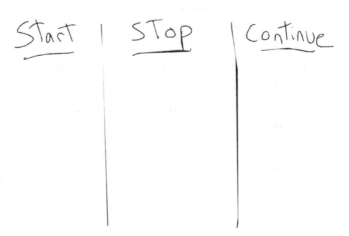

1. Start

What's something new you can introduce to improve your progress? Think about opportunities, tools, or activities that align with your goals.

Example: Start practicing open-ended questions with a peer for 10 minutes every day to boost audience engagement.

2. Stop

What's not serving you? Identify time wasters or low-value activities that you can let go of to free up energy for what matters most.

Example: Stop using that generic presentation book if it doesn't help you engage your audience.

3. Continue

What's working well? Keep doing the things that are driving results and consider how you might enhance them even further.

Example: If practicing open-ended questions with a peer is effective, increase the frequency or refine your approach for even better results.

What I love about the Start, Stop, Continue method is its simplicity. All you need to do is draw three columns labeled Start, Stop, and Continue.

Self-Reflection Question

What's one strategy you've been holding onto that might not be serving you anymore? How can letting it go free up space for something new?

Immediate Action Step

Take a moment to think about your journey so far:

- What should you start doing to improve?
- What should you stop doing to save time or avoid inefficiencies?
- What should you continue doing to build on your success?

Write your answers in the Start, Stop, Continue chart, and set a reminder to revisit it in two weeks. Adjusting your strategies is all about working smarter, not harder. By regularly evaluating what to start, stop, and continue, you can focus on what works, let go of what doesn't, and embrace new ideas with confidence.

Prompt to Share with Your Peer Network

Share your reflections using the Start, Stop, Continue method in a supportive community.

Share one action from each column (Start, Stop, Continue) and explain why you chose them. Invite others to share their thoughts or suggest additional strategies to refine your approach.

Comment on others' posts and exchange ideas for mutual growth.

Closing Thought

Success isn't about perfection—it's about persistence and adaptability. Each adjustment you make brings you closer to your goals. Embrace the process, and trust that the path to growth is built one smart decision at a time.

18
BUILDING A STRONG SUPPORT SYSTEM

Have you ever felt like you're facing challenges alone, without anyone to lean on or turn to for advice?

Success doesn't have to be a solo journey, and a strong support system can make all the difference. The right people and connections can be game-changers for your career and personal growth, while the absence of support can feel like walking through quicksand. Without a strong network, struggles feel heavier, opportunities seem out of reach, and progress becomes unnecessarily slow.

My Struggle with a Weak Support System

I've been there. Throughout most of my career, I thought I had to do everything on my own to prove myself. I didn't want to bother anyone or appear weak, so I kept my struggles to myself. It was exhausting. Without people to brainstorm with or structured feedback loops, I often felt stuck and unsure if I was making the right moves.

I remember one night when I was juggling two major deadlines. I spent hours rewriting the same section of a report, second-guessing every detail. A quick chat with a mentor could have clarified everything, but instead, I spent the entire evening spiraling in self-doubt. Worse, when I finally launched the project, it was clear I'd missed critical elements—things a mentor or colleague might have spotted right away. The frustration of wasted time and effort was overwhelming, and I vowed to never let myself struggle in isolation again.

The Turning Point

Everything changed when I started intentionally building my support system. I reached out to mentors, joined professional groups, and began leaning on trusted colleagues. Suddenly, I wasn't alone. Problems became easier to solve with fresh perspectives, and the encouragement I received gave me the confidence to tackle bigger challenges. A strong support system didn't just lighten my load—it accelerated my growth.

How Support Systems Make a Difference

A strong support system offers more than just encouragement—it provides actionable benefits that can transform how you approach challenges and opportunities.

1. Boosting Confidence

When you're facing challenges or doubting yourself, having people who believe in you can make all the difference. A mentor's reassurance or a friend's pep talk can remind you of your strengths and keep you moving forward.

2. Solving Problems

Sometimes, we get stuck in our own heads. A diverse network can bring fresh perspectives and innovative solutions to your challenges. Whether it's a brainstorming session with colleagues or advice from a mentor, you'll find new ways to tackle obstacles.

3. Staying Accountable

Sharing your goals with someone creates accountability. Whether it's a coach, a peer, or a success buddy, knowing that someone's rooting for you helps you stay on track and committed.

4. Creating Opportunities

Your network can open doors you didn't even know existed. From job referrals to leadership roles, the people you connect with can help you access opportunities that align with your dreams.

5. Building Resilience and Well-Being

Life isn't always smooth sailing. When setbacks happen, having people to lean on—whether it's friends, family, or a supportive community—can help you bounce back stronger.

Examples of Support Systems

Support can come from all kinds of places. Here are some examples:

- **Professional:** Mentors, colleagues, industry associations, and online professional communities.

- **Personal:** Friends, family, and social groups that provide emotional and practical support.

For example, a mentor from your industry might help you refine your goals, while a close friend could offer emotional support during tough times. The best support systems blend personal and professional connections, creating a strong foundation that has your back no matter what.

 ### Self-Reflection Question

What's one area of your life or career where you feel unsupported? How can you take a step toward building or strengthening a support system in that area?

 ### Immediate Action Step

Take 15 minutes to reflect on your current network:

1. **Who's in it?** List the people and groups who support you right now.

Are there gaps? Identify areas where you feel unsupported—for example, do you lack a mentor or accountability partner?

 ### Prompt to Share with Your Peer Network

Building a support system is a collective effort. Share your reflections with your community:

Share one way your support system has helped you grow and one area where you're looking to strengthen connections. Invite others to share how they've built their own support systems and what strategies worked best for them.

Celebrate the value of community by commenting on others' posts and offering encouragement.

Closing Thought

Your support system is the foundation for growth, resilience, and success. It gives you the confidence to tackle challenges, the accountability to stay on track, and the resilience to keep going when things get tough. Start small, reach out, and build connections that will carry you forward. You don't have to do this alone—and with the right people by your side, you'll go further than you ever thought possible.

19

BUILDING YOUR MENTORSHIP NETWORK

What if you had a team of people rooting for your success, each bringing unique perspectives to help you navigate your career?

That's the power of a mentorship network—and it's closer to your reach than you might think. Mentorship is one of the most powerful ways to accelerate your progress.

But here's the twist: it doesn't have to come from just one person. A mentorship network—a team of mentors with different strengths and perspectives—can give you the guidance and opportunities you need to thrive. In this chapter, we'll explore what a mentorship network is, why it matters, and how to build one that truly works for you.

Why Most of Us Struggle with Mentorship

When I first thought about finding a mentor, I assumed I needed one perfect person—someone who would have all the answers and guide me through every challenge. That belief set me up for frustration. I reached out to someone I admired, but the relationship didn't click the way I hoped. It wasn't their fault; I was expecting them to fill every role instead of recognizing the value of a broader mentorship network.

Many of us fall into this trap. We look for a single mentor to be our career GPS, only to be disappointed when they can't meet all our needs. The truth is career growth is too complex for one person to guide us entirely. That's why creating a mentorship network is such a game-changer—it distributes the load and gives you access to a wealth of knowledge, perspectives, and support.

What Is a Mentorship Network?

A mentorship network is like assembling your own personal board of advisors, with each person offering unique advice and perspectives. Here are the four key types of mentors to include in your network:

- **Traditional Mentor:** This is a seasoned professional who provides big-picture guidance and long-term career advice. They've walked the path you're on and can help you avoid common pitfalls. For example, a senior executive might help you strategize your next career move or provide insights on leadership challenges.

- **Peer Mentor:** A peer mentor is someone at a similar stage in their career who understands the challenges you're facing. They can provide relatable advice, act as a sounding board, and brainstorm solutions with you. For instance, a coworker who is also navigating a leadership role could share strategies that have worked for them.

- **Reverse Mentor:** This is someone younger or newer to your field who brings fresh, innovative ideas and challenges traditional thinking. A tech-savvy junior colleague might introduce you to new tools or ways of working that you hadn't considered, helping you stay current in a rapidly evolving industry.

- **Virtual Mentor:** These are experts who inspire and guide you indirectly through their content, such as books, podcasts, videos, or online courses. Following thought leaders in your industry or engaging with their resources can provide valuable insights and keep you motivated.

By diversifying your network with these different types of mentors, you gain a broader range of perspectives, ensuring your growth journey is well-rounded and adaptable.

Why a Mentorship Network Matters

Building a mentorship network is like unlocking a treasure chest of career growth tools. Imagine having a team of people who genuinely care about your success, each bringing their unique strengths and perspectives to the table. It's not just helpful—it's transformative.

Mentors accelerate your growth by sharing their experiences, helping you avoid common pitfalls, and offering actionable advice. For example, when I was preparing for a big presentation, my peer mentor helped refine my messaging, my reverse mentor introduced a new tool for visual storytelling, and my traditional mentor gave me the confidence to deliver it boldly. Together, they turned a daunting challenge into a successful milestone.

Beyond that, mentorship networks provide diverse perspectives that reshape how you approach problems. Your traditional mentor might focus on long-term strategy, while your reverse mentor highlights cutting-edge tools. These different viewpoints ensure you're not just solving problems but innovating solutions.

Mentors also open doors. Whether it's connecting you to key opportunities, championing you for leadership roles, or expanding your visibility within the industry, they're often the catalysts for career-changing moments. Most importantly, mentors are there when things get tough. They remind you of your strengths and encourage you to keep going, building your resilience for the journey ahead.

How to Build Your Mentorship Network

Creating a strong mentorship network might sound daunting, but it's simpler than you think. Here are the steps to get started:

1. **Reflect on Your Needs**
   Start by clarifying your goals. What skills do you want to develop? What challenges are you facing? Who could provide guidance in these areas? This reflection will help you identify the type of mentors you need.

2. **Identify Potential Mentors**
   Look for mentors in various categories—traditional, peer, reverse, and virtual. Use platforms like LinkedIn to search for professionals who align with your goals. Professional associations, online communities, and local events are also excellent places to connect with potential mentors.

3. **Make the Ask**
   Reaching out can feel intimidating, but most people enjoy sharing their knowledge. When you approach someone, be specific and respectful of their time. For example, ask for a short meeting to learn about their journey and seek advice. Personalize your message to show genuine interest in their work.

4. **Nurture Relationships**
   Mentorship is about building meaningful connections. Show appreciation for their guidance, act on their advice, and keep them updated on your progress. Find ways to give back by sharing insights or recommending resources.

5. **Evaluate and Expand**
   As your career evolves, your mentorship needs will change. Regularly assess your network to ensure it aligns with your current goals. Don't hesitate to add new mentors as needed to keep your support system dynamic and relevant.

Self-Reflection Question

Who in your life has already acted as a mentor, even informally? How can you strengthen that relationship or show gratitude for their guidance?

Immediate Action Step
Identify one person for each type of mentor:

- **Traditional Mentor:** Who can provide big-picture guidance?
- **Peer Mentor:** Who understands your challenges and can offer relatable advice?
- **Reverse Mentor:** Who brings fresh perspectives and innovative ideas?
- **Virtual Mentor:** What thought leaders or resources inspire you?

Reach out to one potential mentor this week. Take the first step toward creating your network.

Prompt to Share with Your Peer Network
Mentorship networks thrive when shared. Here's how to engage with your community:

Share what type of mentor you're seeking and why.

Share a positive experience with a mentor to inspire others to build their networks.

Invite peers to suggest potential mentors or resources.

Closing Thought

Your mentorship network is your secret weapon for career growth. By connecting with a diverse group of mentors, you'll gain the guidance, insights, and opportunities you need to thrive. Start small, be intentional, and watch your network grow into a powerful force for your success. Your journey begins with one conversation—take that step today.

20

THE POWER OF PEER SUPPORT AND ONLINE COMMUNITIES

When it comes to career growth, peer support and online communities are like rocket fuel.

They connect you with people who get it—like-minded individuals who understand your goals, your challenges, and your determination to succeed. Imagine having a group of people to turn to for advice, celebrate milestones with, and lean on during challenges. That's the power of peer support: it turns an uphill climb into a team effort.

How Peer Support Differs from a Mentorship Network

Before diving into peer support, let's differentiate it from mentorship, which we covered in the previous chapter. While mentorship offers guidance from individuals with varying experience levels, peer support focuses on collaboration and mutual growth among those on a similar journey. Think of your mentorship network as strategic advisors and your peer network as daily teammates, working together to propel you forward.

- **Mentorship Network:** Provides a variety of perspectives, from seasoned professionals to fresh innovators, to guide your long-term career strategy and development.

- **Peer Network:** Offers day-to-day support, shared experiences, and real-time feedback from people facing similar challenges and goals.

For instance, a mentorship network might help you envision and strategize your next career move, drawing wisdom from individuals who have already navigated those waters. In contrast, a peer network gives you immediate, relatable insights and accountability—whether it's brainstorming solutions to a specific problem or celebrating milestones together.

Core Elements of Peer Support

Peer support isn't just helpful—it's energizing. Here are the key elements that make it powerful:

- **Advice:** Swapping tips and insights that actually work. Peers can offer real-world solutions tailored to your challenges because they're experiencing similar hurdles.

- **Support:** Cheering each other on through challenges and setbacks. Having a network to turn to during tough times can make obstacles feel manageable.

- **Accountability:** Keeping each other on track and motivated to crush goals. Knowing you're reporting progress to someone else can drive consistency and commitment.

Together, these elements remind you that you're not alone and that collaboration can accelerate progress far beyond what's possible individually.

Why Online Communities Elevate Peer Support

Online communities amplify the benefits of peer support by connecting you with a wider network of individuals who share your ambitions. They're hubs of shared knowledge, encouragement, and collaboration that are accessible anytime, anywhere. For example, platforms like LinkedIn groups or Slack workspaces allow you to tap into industry-specific expertise and connect with professionals who face similar challenges.

Key Benefits of Online Communities:

- **Shared Knowledge:** Imagine joining a group of professionals where someone has already solved the exact problem you're facing. Their insights save you time and give you practical solutions you can apply immediately.

- **Emotional Support:** These communities create safe spaces where you can share struggles and celebrate successes without judgment. Knowing others understand your journey and have your back can be a powerful motivator.

- **Accountability and Motivation:** When you share your goals with a community, you're inviting others to help keep you on track. Seeing your peers hit milestones can spark your own determination to keep pushing forward.

Online communities don't just connect you to people—they connect you to possibilities. The relationships you build and the resources you discover can elevate your career in ways you never imagined.

What to Look For, and What to Avoid

Not every online group will be the right fit, so it's important to choose wisely. Here's a checklist to help you maximize the impact:

- **Look For:**
  - Groups that align with your goals and values.
  - Career-focused communities like The Top 10% Club,

designed to keep you inspired and on track without unnecessary distractions.

- o Industry-specific groups tailored to your trade, skill, or professional niche for targeted advice and connections.

- **Avoid:**
  - o Toxic or unproductive spaces where negativity overshadows growth.
  - o Platforms overloaded with unrelated content that pulls you away from your goals.

Once you've found the right groups, don't just lurk—jump into discussions! Ask questions, share your wins, and offer advice when you can. Engagement is key to building meaningful connections and reaping the benefits of peer support.

Self-Reflection Question

Who in your current network has provided valuable support or advice recently? How can you express gratitude or deepen that connection?

Immediate Action Step

Take 15 minutes to reflect on your current network of online communities. Ask yourself:

Are they helping you grow? Are they offering the support, advice, and accountability you need? What changes could you make?

Maybe it's time to find a new group or engage more deeply in the ones that are working for you. Write down one step you can take this week to strengthen your peer network.

 **Prompt to Share with Your Peer Network**

Peer networks thrive on active participation. Here's how you can engage:

Share what you're working on and why it matters to you. Invite others to share their experiences or tips related to your challenges.

Share a recent success, no matter how small, and encourage others to do the same.

Closing Thought

Peer support and online communities are more than just networks—they're accelerators of growth, resilience, and success. Surrounding yourself with like-minded individuals who share your goals and challenges transforms your journey from a solo climb to a team effort. Take the time to evaluate your current connections, engage meaningfully, and seek out communities that inspire you to reach new heights. Together, there's no limit to what you can achieve.

21
THE POWER OF LOCAL ASSOCIATIONS AND MEETUPS

While online communities are amazing for connection and support, face-to-face interactions offer a unique opportunity to build deeper connections and foster personal growth.

Local associations and meetups bring a level of personal engagement that can strengthen relationships, spark new opportunities, and fuel your growth. For example, attending a local industry meetup could lead to discovering a mentor, learning about new job openings, or collaborating on projects that align with your goals.

Why Local Groups Are Different from Online Communities

Before diving into the benefits of local associations and meetups, let's take a moment to understand how they differ from online communities. Both offer valuable support and networking opportunities, but the dynamics are distinct.

- **Depth of Connection:** In-person interactions allow for deeper, more authentic connections. A handshake, shared laugh, or eye contact creates a bond that's hard to replicate online.

- **Immediate Feedback:** Whether you're practicing a pitch or brainstorming ideas, in-person groups offer real-time responses that help you refine and improve.

- **Local Relevance:** These groups focus on opportunities and challenges specific to your area, making the connections and advice more directly applicable.

While online communities provide global access and convenience, local groups excel at fostering genuine relationships and hands-on collaboration.

The Unique Benefits of Local Groups

These in-person groups offer something that online communities often can't: the power of personal interaction.

1. Access to Mentors

Learn from seasoned professionals eager to share their knowledge. Mentors you meet in these spaces provide personalized guidance, offering advice rooted in their own experiences and tailored specifically to help you navigate your unique challenges.

2. Peer Connections

Meeting people who share your challenges and aspirations can be incredibly energizing. Regular face-to-face interactions build a strong sense of community and accountability, creating momentum and support for consistent growth.

3. Opportunities for Leadership

Local groups are often hotbeds for new roles, collaborative projects, and leadership experiences. Taking on a leadership role in an association not only boosts your professional profile but also deepens your skill set in ways that prepare you for bigger career moves. For example, stepping into a leadership role within an industry group can showcase your commitment and enhance your visibility.

4. Inspiration and Growth

Face-to-face encouragement hits differently—it's genuine, immediate, and deeply motivating. For instance, attending a meetup where industry leaders share success stories can ignite fresh ideas and inspire bold action in your own journey.

Overcoming the Initial Hesitation

The idea of joining a local association or meetup can feel intimidating, especially when you're stepping into a space where you might not know anyone or feel out of place. For many, it's not just about finding the time but confronting the fear of stepping into an unfamiliar space. What if you don't know anyone? What if you don't feel like you belong?

Everyone feels this way at first, but the rewards of stepping out of your comfort zone far outweigh the initial discomfort. The key is to remember that local groups are designed to be welcoming spaces for people just like you. Whether you're an industry newcomer or a seasoned professional, these communities thrive on shared goals and mutual support.

Consider starting small by attending a casual networking event or reaching out to one person in the group for a conversation.

How to Get Started

Joining a local group is easier than you think. Here's how you can take the first step:

- **Identify Relevant Associations:** Look for groups that align with your career goals, interests, or skills. Use Google, community boards, or platforms like Meetup to find associations and events in your area.

- **Get Involved:** Attend meetings, introduce yourself, and actively participate in discussions. Focus on building genuine relationships by showing interest in others and engaging authentically—connections thrive on sincerity. Share your knowledge and contribute to the group to create mutual value.

- **Start Your Own Group:** Can't find a group that fits your needs? Start one yourself! Whether it's a niche professional meetup or a skill-specific association, creating a group will attract like-minded individuals who share your goals.

Self-Reflection Question

What's one local group or association you've been curious about but haven't joined yet? What's holding you back, and how can you overcome that hesitation?

Immediate Action Step

Take 15 minutes to reflect on your current engagement with local groups. Are there opportunities you've overlooked or events you've been meaning to attend?

Now is the perfect time to take action.

Prompt to Share with Your Peer Network

Community thrives on shared experiences. Share your thoughts with your network:

Share the local group you're considering joining and why it excites you. Invite your peers to suggest associations or meetups they've found valuable.

If you've recently attended a local event, share your takeaways and encourage others to join similar groups.

Closing Thought

Local associations and meetups offer more than networking—they offer connection, growth, and opportunity. By stepping into these spaces, you're investing in relationships that can shape your career and inspire your personal development. Whether you're attending your first meeting or stepping into a leadership role, these in-person interactions have the power to transform your journey. Take that first step—the rewards are waiting.

22
MAXIMIZING YOUR MOST PRECIOUS RESOURCE

Imagine what you could achieve if every hour of your day was spent intentionally moving closer to your goals.

Time is your most precious resource. Unlike money or possessions, you can't make more of it, so how you use it matters more than anything else. That's where time optimization comes in. It's not just about managing your time—it's about prioritizing what truly matters, cutting out distractions, and taking consistent steps toward your goals.

The Trap of Poor Time Management

Time optimization sounds great in theory, but in practice, it's tough. Most of us get stuck in cycles of busyness, mistaking activity for productivity. Have you ever had a day packed with tasks but ended up feeling like you didn't accomplish anything meaningful? That's the trap of poor time management. We fill our schedules with low-priority tasks, get distracted by notifications, or procrastinate on what really matters.

The key to breaking free? Shifting your mindset. Time optimization isn't about doing more—it's about doing what matters most.

Why Time Optimization Matters in Skill Mastery

We all have the same 24 hours in a day, but how you use them makes all the difference. Optimizing your time means choosing to spend it on what moves you closer to your dreams instead of getting sidetracked by unimportant tasks.

For skill mastery, this is particularly crucial. Without intentional focus, your time can be consumed by distractions that pull you away from consistent progress. Recognizing that your time is limited empowers you to prioritize your learning and practice, ensuring every moment is purposeful.

The Benefits of Time Optimization

Time optimization creates a foundation for meaningful progress. Here's why it's a game-changer:

- **Consistent Progress:** Small, regular actions create momentum and lead to big results over time. For example, spending just 20 focused minutes daily on skill mastery adds up to over 120 hours a year—enough to become proficient in almost any skill.

- **Reduced Stress:** Having control over your schedule helps you avoid overcommitment and chaos. For instance, Sarah, a project manager, used time optimization to reduce her workload from 60 hours a week to 45 while delivering even better results.

- **Focused Practice:** Spending your time intentionally accelerates your growth and helps you see results faster. Skill mastery thrives on deep, uninterrupted focus, and time optimization ensures you can dedicate those precious hours to improving your craft.

When you optimize your time for skill mastery, you create an environment where learning becomes a priority, progress feels tangible, and your efforts are aligned with your long-term goals.

Taking a Hard Look at Your Time

Before you can optimize your time, you need to understand how you're currently using it. Most of us don't realize just how much of our day is eaten up by distractions or low-value tasks.

It's easy to feel busy without being productive, and that's where the real challenge lies. How often do you find yourself scrolling through social media, sitting in unproductive meetings, or tackling tasks that don't align with your goals? These moments add up, stealing time from the activities that truly matter. Taking a clear-eyed look at your schedule is the first step to reclaiming those hours and putting them to better use.

Self-Reflection Question

What's one activity you can stop doing this week to reclaim 15 minutes a day for skill mastery?

Immediate Action Step

Here's a simple exercise to start optimizing your time:

1. For one day, log everything you do—every task, every break, every distraction.

2. At the end of the day, analyze your log. Highlight tasks that don't align with your goals or consume more time than they should have.

This awareness is a powerful motivator to make meaningful changes and reclaim your time for what truly matters.

Prompt to Share with Your Peer Network

Your insights on time optimization can inspire and motivate others. Here's how to share:

Share what you learned from tracking your time and what changes you plan to make. Invite your network to share their favorite time optimization strategies.

Partner with a peer to hold each other accountable for staying focused on high-priority tasks.

Closing Thought

Time optimization isn't about working harder; it's about working smarter. By focusing your energy on what matters most and eliminating distractions, you create the conditions for consistent, meaningful progress. Every decision to prioritize what matters most brings you closer to the version of yourself you aspire to be. Start today—your future self will thank you.

23
PRIORITIZATION: FOCUSING ON WHAT MATTERS MOST

Imagine this: You've been working nonstop all day, crossing tasks off your list, but when the day ends, you feel like you've accomplished nothing meaningful.

Sound familiar? You're not alone. The constant feeling of being busy without meaningful progress can lead to burnout, diminished confidence, and even resentment toward your work or goals.

Without a clear plan, everything feels urgent. You end up juggling too many tasks and dropping the ball on the ones that matter most. By focusing on the wrong things, you miss out on high-impact activities that could propel you forward. Low-priority tasks take up valuable time, leaving little room for the meaningful work that drives growth. Over time, the pressure of unfinished to-dos and unproductive days chips away at your motivation and well-being.

The solution? **Prioritization.** When you focus on what truly matters, you're not just managing your time—you're creating a life aligned with your goals.

The Eisenhower Matrix: Your Priority-Setting Blueprint

Thankfully, there's a proven method to cut through the clutter and bring clarity to your day: the Eisenhower Matrix. By categorizing your tasks based on urgency and importance, you gain clarity on what deserves your attention right now.

Understanding the Quadrants

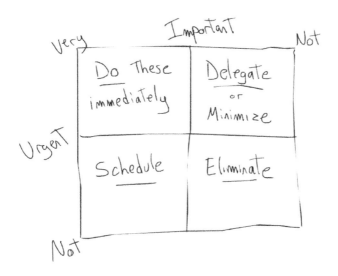

1. **Urgent & Important (Do):** These are tasks that require immediate attention and are critical to your success. Examples include meeting deadlines, resolving crises, or handling pressing client needs. These are your top priorities—handle them right away.

2. **Urgent but Not Important (Delegate):** Tasks in this category must be completed quickly but don't require your personal involvement. Examples include scheduling meetings, routine emails, or administrative work. Delegate, automate, or streamline these tasks so you can focus on higher-impact priorities.

3. **Not Urgent & Not Important (Eliminate):** These are time wasters that don't contribute to your goals. Think of tasks like

mindlessly scrolling social media or attending unnecessary meetings. Eliminate these to free up valuable time.

4. **Not Urgent but Important (Schedule):** This is the goldmine quadrant. These tasks might not demand immediate attention but are critical for long-term success and growth. Examples include mastering a skill, strategic planning, building relationships, or self-care. Schedule these tasks and treat them as sacred time blocks.

How to Use the Eisenhower Matrix Effectively

Step 1: Reflect on Your Tasks

Start by listing everything on your plate. Include big projects, small to-dos, and even the tasks you've been avoiding. Then categorize each task into one of the four quadrants of the matrix.

Step 2: Eliminate or Delegate

Look at the tasks in the "Not Urgent & Not Important" quadrant. Start removing these from your day—they're time-sinks with no real value. Next, identify tasks in the "Urgent but Not Important" quadrant that can be delegated or automated.

Step 3: Schedule What Matters

Protect time for "Not Urgent but Important" tasks. These are the activities that build your future. Block time on your calendar to work on them consistently. Treat these time blocks as sacred—don't let distractions sneak in.

Self-Reflection Question

What's one "Not Urgent & Not Important" task you can eliminate this week? How will removing it open time for activities that align with your goals?

 ### Immediate Action Step

Take a moment to start identifying where your daily actions fall into the Eisenhower Matrix. Look at your tasks and categorize each into one of the four quadrants:

- ✓ **Urgent & Important (Do):** What tasks absolutely need immediate attention?
- ✓ **Urgent but Not Important (Delegate):** Which tasks can someone else handle for you?
- ✓ **Not Urgent & Not Important (Eliminate):** Where are you wasting time with little to no value added?
- ✓ **Not Urgent but Important (Schedule):** What activities are essential to your long-term goals but need dedicated focus?

This step is all about clarity. Don't worry yet about eliminating or delegating tasks—focus on awareness and sorting your actions.

 ### Prompt to Share with Your Peer Network

Your prioritization journey can inspire others. Here's how to share:

Share your insights on how you're using the Eisenhower Matrix to sort your tasks. Invite your network to suggest tips for better time prioritization.

Partner with a peer to keep each other accountable for focusing on high-impact activities.

Closing Thought

The Eisenhower Matrix is more than a productivity tool—it's a way to reclaim your time and align your life with what truly matters. By choosing to prioritize with intention, you're not just managing your day—you're creating a future filled with purpose and progress. Remember, success isn't about doing it all; it's about doing what counts. Start prioritizing today—your future self will thank you.

24
MINIMIZING ACTIVITIES THAT MATTER LEAST

Ever feel like you're constantly busy, yet at the end of the day, it's hard to pinpoint what you've truly accomplished?

I remember one particular week when I worked tirelessly on several projects. My calendar was packed, my email inbox was overflowing, and I barely had time to catch my breath. By Friday evening, I realized I had spent most of my time answering messages and attending unproductive meetings. Despite being "busy" all week, I couldn't name a single task that had truly moved me closer to my goals.

If this sounds familiar, you're not alone. These time wasters are sneaky but recognizing them is the first step to taking back control. The good news? You have the power to take control and reclaim your time.

By identifying and addressing these low-value activities, you can create space for the work that truly matters—the tasks that fuel your growth, align with your goals, and bring you closer to success.

The Cost of Ignoring Time Wasters

When you let time wasters persist, the consequences add up:

- **Lost Focus:** Constant interruptions pull you away from meaningful work, making it harder to concentrate and produce quality results.

- **Overwhelm:** Low-priority tasks leave little mental energy for what truly matters, creating a sense of chaos.

- **Delayed Progress:** Every minute spent on distractions is a minute not spent on your goals, pushing back your growth timeline.

- **Burnout:** The stress of being busy without making real progress can leave you drained and unmotivated.

Recognizing these patterns is the first step toward change. Let's dive into some of the most common culprits.

Common Time Wasters

We've all encountered these sneaky productivity killers. Here are some of the biggest offenders:

- **Email Overload:** Spending hours in your inbox, responding to every notification, can leave you stuck in reactive mode. Imagine spending 30 minutes drafting an email that could be resolved with a quick 2-minute phone call.

- **Unproductive Meetings:** Without clear agendas or actionable outcomes, meetings often turn into time sinks. Think about the last meeting where nothing meaningful was decided—it's a common frustration.

- **Low-Priority Administrative Tasks:** Organizing files, filling out forms, or scheduling appointments may feel productive, but they rarely make a significant impact.

- **Multitasking:** Juggling multiple tasks may feel efficient, but it often leads to half-finished work and a sense of frustration.

- **Social Media Scrolling:** One quick glance at Instagram can easily turn into 30 minutes lost in a rabbit hole of cat videos. Social media is designed to grab your attention and keep it.

- **Overcommitting:** Saying "yes" to too many things dilutes your focus and spreads your energy too thin, making it impossible to excel.

- **Procrastination:** Avoiding difficult or uncomfortable tasks by doing something easier might feel like a break, but it delays progress and adds unnecessary stress.

3 Strategies to Reclaiming Your Time

Here's how you can take back control of your day.

1. Delegate

Hand off tasks that don't require your unique skills or attention. For example:

- Use scheduling tools like Calendly to automate meeting coordination.
- Assign repetitive tasks like data entry or research to an assistant or junior colleague.

2. Minimize

Streamline unavoidable tasks to make them less disruptive. Examples include:

- Limiting email checks to two focused slots a day—once in the morning and once before signing off.
- Setting strict time limits for meetings, ensuring they stay

focused and productive.

3. Eliminate

Get rid of tasks that add no real value to your goals. For instance:

- Recognize excessive social media scrolling as a "Not Urgent & Not Important" activity and replace it with something more energizing, like a quick walk or a power nap.
- Decline unproductive meetings or busy work that doesn't align with your priorities.

Self-Reflection Question

What's one low-value task you've been holding onto, and how could removing it open up time for meaningful work?

Immediate Action Step

This week, take the first step by identifying the activities that drain your time without adding value.

Choose one task to eliminate, delegate, or minimize this week. Start small and build momentum.

Prompt to Share with Your Peer Network

Your journey to reclaim time can inspire others.

Share a specific time waster you've identified and how you plan to tackle it. Invite your network to share their favorite tips for eliminating distractions.

Collaborate with a peer to exchange strategies and celebrate progress together.

Closing Thought

Minimizing time wasters isn't just about being more productive—it's about reclaiming your energy, focus, and joy. Every moment you free up is an opportunity to invest in the work and relationships that truly matter. By delegating, minimizing, and eliminating these time wasters, you're not just taking control of your schedule—you're taking control of your growth. Start today—your future self will thank you.

25
CREATING A SUSTAINABLE SCHEDULE THAT WORKS FOR YOU

Have you ever looked at your calendar and wondered, "Where did the time go?"

We've all had days where we're busy but not productive. Days filled with back-to-back meetings, endless busy work, and constant interruptions can leave you frustrated and unfulfilled. Without a clear strategy, your schedule ends up controlling you rather than empowering you to achieve your goals.

As we continue to master impactful skills, demands on our time will only grow. This is a good problem to have, but it requires proactive management to avoid burnout and maximize impact. The good news? Creating a schedule that works for you is possible—and it starts with recognizing common pitfalls and adopting strategies that prioritize what truly matters.

Common Scheduling Pitfalls

Even with the best intentions, certain habits can derail your efforts to create an effective schedule. Let's explore the four most common mistakes and how to avoid them:

1. Trying to Do Too Much

Packing your day with too many tasks leaves no room to breathe or adapt. By the evening, you're likely to feel exhausted but unaccomplished. Overcommitting stretches you thin, reduces focus, and diminishes your impact.

2. Neglecting Priorities

Without a clear sense of what's important, it's easy to fill your time with tasks that feel urgent but don't truly matter. For example, spending hours organizing your inbox instead of preparing for an important presentation leads to frustration and disheartening results.

3. Ignoring Self-Care

Skipping meals, working through breaks, and staying up late to finish tasks might seem productive in the moment, but over time, it drains your energy and leads to burnout. Sustainable success requires balancing productivity with personal well-being.

4. Failing to Adjust

Life is unpredictable. Unexpected meetings, emergencies, or even low-energy days can throw you off track. Rigid schedules that don't allow flexibility can lead to frustration and hinder your ability to bounce back when things go awry.

The Power of Time Blocking

Time blocking is a simple yet powerful strategy that ensures your time is spent intentionally. By assigning specific tasks to dedicated time slots, you gain clarity, reduce decision fatigue, and protect your most productive hours for high-impact work.

How Time Blocking Works

1. **Prioritize High-Impact Tasks:** Reserve your peak productivity hours for tasks that matter most. For instance, if

you're sharpest in the morning, dedicate that time to deep work or strategic projects.

2. **Include Breaks and Self-Care:** Schedule time for relaxation, exercise, and connecting with loved ones. These activities recharge your energy and prevent burnout.

3. **Be Consistent:** Set recurring blocks for regular activities like learning, planning, or reflection. Consistency builds habits that drive long-term progress.

Example Time Blocks

- 5–7 AM: Morning self-care (e.g., meditation, stretching, or reading).
- 9–11 AM: Focused work (e.g., strategic projects or deep creative tasks).
- 1–2 PM: Lunch and light exercise.
- 3–5 PM: Meetings or collaborative tasks.
- 7–8 PM: Wind-down routine (e.g., journaling or family time).

Taking It to the Next Level with the Pomodoro Method

Time blocking gives your day structure, but the Pomodoro method takes it further by breaking tasks into manageable chunks. This technique keeps your productivity high while preventing burnout.

How It Works

1. Work for 25 minutes on one task.
2. Take a 5-minute break.
3. Repeat this cycle for 2–3 rounds.
4. After three cycles, take a longer break (20–30 minutes).

Why It Works

The Pomodoro method works because it recognizes the limits of our attention spans and builds in strategic breaks to recharge and refocus. This prevents burnout, boosts focus, and makes even the biggest projects feel manageable.

Example Application

Imagine you're preparing a presentation:

- Cycle 1: Draft the outline.
- Cycle 2: Develop key slides.
- Cycle 3: Practice delivery.
- Long Break: Go for a quick walk or stretch to recharge before final edits.

Self-Reflection Question

What's one adjustment you can make to your schedule this week that would have the biggest impact on your productivity and well-being?

Immediate Action Steps

1. **Create One Time Block:** Start with a morning self-care routine or a focused work session. Commit to doing it daily.

2. **Experiment with Focused Work:** Try short, focused sessions using the Pomodoro method to see how they improve your energy and focus.

3. **Evaluate and Adjust:** Reflect on what works and what doesn't. Make tweaks to your schedule based on your observations.

 **Prompt to Share with Your Peer Network**

Your approach to scheduling can inspire and help others refine their own routines.

Share how you're structuring your day using time blocking or the Pomodoro method. Highlight what's working well and any challenges you've encountered.

Invite peers to share their experiences or suggest strategies for managing their time effectively.

Closing Thought

A sustainable schedule isn't about cramming more into your day— it's about doing what matters most. By prioritizing high-impact tasks, incorporating flexibility, and valuing self-care, you're setting yourself up for long-term success. Remember, progress comes from consistent effort, not perfection. Start building a schedule that works for you today—your future self will thank you.

26
90-DAY SKILL MASTERY PLAN
PHASE 1: FOUNDATIONS (DAYS 1-30)

This is where it all comes together. You've been building up to this moment, and now it's time to turn everything you've learned into action. You're about to create a clear, actionable 90-day plan that will help you master a career-defining skill. This isn't just a to-do list—it's your blueprint for growth, your guide to becoming the best version of yourself.

I remember the first time I tried to create a structured plan for skill mastery. I was excited but overwhelmed by the sheer number of tasks and resources competing for my attention. I didn't know where to start, and I often found myself second-guessing whether I was focusing on the right things. It wasn't until I broke everything down into clear, manageable steps that I started to see real progress. That's exactly what we're going to do here—simplify the process so you can focus on what truly matters.

Let's start with the first 30 days. This is where the foundation is laid, where small, consistent actions pave the way for big, meaningful progress. Ready? Let's go.

Phase 1: Foundations (Days 1-30)
1. Identify a High-Impact Skill

Think about a skill that excites you, feels practical, and can make a real difference in your career. This should be something that sparks your interest and aligns with your goals.

- **Example:** Perhaps you're a team leader who wants to become a more engaging presenter to inspire your colleagues.

Notes:

2. Create a Fire Statement

Your fire statement is your "why"—the deep motivation that will keep you going when things get tough. Revisit what drives you and put it into words.

- **Example:** "I'm motivated to master presenting because I love inspiring people and sharing big ideas that make an impact."

Notes:

3. Pinpoint a Target Competency

Break your chosen skill into smaller areas and pick one to focus on first. This narrows your efforts and makes success more achievable.

- **Example:** If your skill is presenting, you might focus on audience engagement as your first competency.

Notes:

4. Set Measurable Performance Indicators

Define clear goals so you can track your progress and celebrate wins along the way.

- **Example:** "Engage at least 30% of my audience with interactive questions during presentations."

Notes:

5. Gather High-Impact Resources

Equip yourself with tools and materials that are tailored to your chosen skill. The more relevant and actionable, the better.

- **Example Resources:**
  - An online course on public speaking.
  - A book by a renowned presentation coach.
  - YouTube videos featuring TED Talk speakers.

Notes:

6. Build Your Mentorship Network

Don't go it alone. Surround yourself with mentors who can guide and inspire you. Create a mix of perspectives to keep your learning fresh and dynamic:

- **Traditional Mentor:** A seasoned expert who's been where you want to go.

- **Peer Mentor:** Someone at a similar stage who can offer relatable insights.
- **Reverse Mentor:** A less experienced person with fresh ideas and perspectives.
- **Virtual Mentor:** Learn from thought leaders through books, videos, and online content.

Notes:

7. Minimize Time Wasters

Let's be honest—we all have distractions that pull us away from what matters. Identify yours and make a plan to reduce or eliminate them.

- **Example:** Replace social media scrolling with focused practice or learning time.

Notes:

8. Schedule Skill Optimization Time

Block out consistent, distraction-free time to focus on your skill. Consistency is what turns effort into progress.

- **Example Schedule:**
  - 5:00–7:00 AM: Self-care and skill learning—reading, practicing, and refining your techniques.

Notes:

Immediate Action Step

It's time to take action! Write your answers in the notes section under each of these eight action items, or download a printable worksheet at https://www.top10percentclub.com/90dayplan

Closing Thought

The first 30 days are all about setting the stage. By identifying your focus, gathering the right resources, and creating a plan, you're building a foundation that will support your growth for the full 90-day journey and beyond. Remember, every small action you take now is an investment in the person you're becoming. Progress isn't about perfection—it's about showing up consistently and adapting as you learn. Start strong—you've got this!

27
90-DAY SKILL MASTERY PLAN
PHASE 2: ACTIVE APPLICATION (DAYS 31-60)

Congratulations! You've done the hard work of laying a solid foundation—now it's time to level up. Welcome to the second phase of your 90-day skill mastery journey: Active Application.

I remember when I first reached this point in my own skill-building journey. I was excited about the progress I'd made, but I quickly realized that preparation and planning weren't enough—I needed to put those ideas into action. One particular project stood out. I had practiced endlessly for a presentation, but the first time I tested my audience engagement techniques, it didn't go as planned. The questions I asked fell flat, and I felt discouraged. But instead of giving up, I adjusted my approach, sought feedback, and tried again. By the third attempt, my audience participation had tripled. This phase is where the seeds you've planted begin to sprout—consistency and care will determine how far you grow. The more consistently you show up, the more momentum you build.

Ready to see some measurable results? Let's dive in.

Phase 2: Active Application (Days 31-60)

1. Test High-Impact Resources
Not every resource will be a perfect fit, and that's okay. Now's the

time to figure out what's working and adjust as needed.

- **What to Do:** Evaluate the books, courses, videos, or tools you've been using. Double down on what resonates and ditch what doesn't.
- **Example:** If online courses and videos feel more engaging than books, shift your focus to those.

Notes:

2. Track Performance Indicators

Perfection isn't the goal here—progress is. Even small wins add up over time.

- **What to Do:** Practice your skill daily for 5–15 minutes and keep track of your progress.
- **Example:** Measure audience engagement during presentations. Start with 10% participation, then aim for 12%, 15%, and beyond.

Notes:

3. Apply Proven Skill Development Strategies

This is where science meets practice. Use these tried-and-true methods to supercharge your learning:

- **Focused Practice:** Zero in on one specific area of your skill at a time.
- **Spaced Repetition:** Revisit key concepts regularly to reinforce them.
- **Active Learning:** Get hands-on, experiment, and learn through doing.

Notes:

4. Engage in Peer Collaboration

You don't have to do this alone. Working with others can provide new perspectives and help you refine your approach.

- **What to Do:** Practice with peers who can offer constructive feedback.
- **Example:** Schedule one-on-one sessions to test audience engagement techniques and get immediate input.

Notes:

5. Refine Time Optimization

Your schedule is your secret weapon. Adjust it to make sure it supports intentional practice and self-care.

- **What to Do:** Add or tweak time blocks to keep your energy high and your practice effective.
- **Example:** Incorporate a midday recharge activity, like a short run or meditation, to stay sharp.

Notes:

6. Seek Feedback Regularly

Think of feedback as your compass. It helps you stay on course and fine-tune your efforts.

- **What to Do:** Ask mentors, peers, or supervisors for specific, actionable input.
- **Example:** A colleague might suggest tweaking your phrasing during presentations to better connect with your audience.

Notes:

7. Share Progress in the Community

Accountability can be a game-changer. Sharing your journey keeps you motivated and inspires others.

- **What to Do:** Post updates in the Top 10% Club community at least three times a week and engage with other members.
- **Example Post:** "This week, I practiced asking interactive questions during presentations. My engagement rate improved from 10% to 15%! Any tips for boosting it even more?"

Notes:

8. Reflect on Midpoint Achievements

You've made it to Day 60—a huge milestone! Take a moment to celebrate how far you've come and make adjustments for the road ahead.

- **Use the Start, Stop, Continue Framework:**
  - **Start:** Experimenting with new strategies or resources.
  - **Stop:** Dropping methods that aren't yielding results.
  - **Continue:** Building on what's working well.

Notes:

Immediate Action Step

It's time to take action! Write your answers in the notes section under each of these eight action items, or download a printable worksheet at https://www.top10percentclub.com/90dayplan

Final Thoughts

This phase is where your hard work starts to pay off. Consistent practice leads to noticeable improvement, feedback helps you refine your approach and identify growth opportunities, and sharing your journey keeps you motivated and connected to your goals. As you continue to apply what you've learned, you'll find that each step builds on the last, creating unstoppable momentum. Keep showing up, keep refining, and keep believing in your ability to grow.

28
90-DAY SKILL MASTERY PLAN
PHASE 3: REFINE AND MASTERY (DAYS 61-90)

You've made it! The final phase of your 90-day skill mastery journey is here. This is where all the effort, focus, and practice come together to create something truly remarkable. Over the next 30 days, you'll refine your skill, tackle high-pressure situations, and step into mastery.

I remember reaching this phase during one of my own skill mastery challenges. I'd been working on honing my presentation skills, and a pivotal moment came when I was asked to deliver a talk to a room full of senior leaders. It was high stakes, and I knew it was my chance to put everything I'd learned into action. I spent hours practicing, refining, and seeking feedback. When the day came, it wasn't perfect, but the progress I'd made was undeniable. I walked away feeling accomplished and energized to push even further.

This phase is your grand finale—a time to shine and cement everything you've worked so hard to achieve. Let's take all that momentum you've built and turn it into your superpower. You're ready for this!

Phase 3: Refine and Mastery (Days 61-90)

1. Compare Progress to Performance Indicators

Take a moment to look back and see how far you've come. Remember those goals you set in Phase 1? It's time to see how you measure up.

- **What to Do:** Revisit your original benchmarks and assess your progress.
- **Example:** If your audience engagement started at 5% and is now at 15%, celebrate! Then, figure out what made the difference and refine your strategies to push even further.

Notes:

2. Focus on Advanced Techniques

This is your opportunity to elevate your game. Now that you've got the basics down, it's time to learn the advanced moves.

- **What to Do:** Explore high-level strategies that can take your skill to the next level.
- **Example:** Research expert-level questioning techniques or storytelling methods to deepen audience engagement. Use AI tools or seek out thought leaders for cutting-edge insights.

Notes:

3. Apply Skills in High-Stakes Scenarios

Mastery happens when you step out of your comfort zone and test your abilities under pressure. This is where growth accelerates.

- **What to Do:** Seek out challenging opportunities to apply your skill.
- **Example:** Deliver a presentation to senior executives or speak at an industry conference. The stakes are high, but so are the rewards.

Notes:

4. Strengthen Mentor Relationships

Your mentors have guided you this far, but there's still more they can offer. Use this phase to deepen those connections and seek higher-level advice.

- **What to Do:** Reach out to mentors with advanced expertise and ask for their insights.
- **Example:** Connect with top presenters or leaders in your field for personalized feedback and inspiration.

Notes:

5. Finalize Time Optimization

By now, you've fine-tuned a schedule that works for you. Use this time to make final adjustments and ensure it's sustainable for the long haul.

- **What to Do:** Lock in your most productive routines while leaving space for reflection and renewal.
- **Example:** Add a reflective evening block to journal your progress and set intentions for the next day.

Notes:

6. Prepare for Skill Demonstration

This is your moment to show the world what you've accomplished. Demonstrating your skill builds confidence and opens doors.

- **What to Do:** Look for opportunities to showcase your

progress.

- **Example:** Join a local Toastmasters group, lead a workshop at work, or volunteer to present at an industry event.

Notes:

7. Document Lessons Learned

Reflection is where the magic happens. Documenting your journey helps you solidify what you've learned and prepares you for future growth.

- **What to Do:** Keep a journal of your challenges, breakthroughs, and key takeaways.
- **Example:** Write about how specific feedback transformed your approach or how advanced techniques improved your performance. Include gratitude for the progress you've made.

Notes:

8. Celebrate Achievements

You've earned this. Recognize your hard work and take a moment to enjoy the results of your dedication.

- **What to Do:** Plan a celebration that feels meaningful to you.
- **Example:** Treat yourself to a special dinner, a weekend getaway, or a reward that symbolizes your accomplishment. Use this celebration to energize your next steps.

Notes:

Immediate Action Step

It's time to take action! Write your answers in the notes section under each of these eight action items, or download a printable worksheet at https://www.top10percentclub.com/90dayplan

Final Thoughts

This phase is where your efforts truly shine. By leaning into advanced techniques, stepping up in high-stakes scenarios, and reflecting on your journey, you've not only mastered a skill but also transformed how you approach growth.

The confidence you've built, the insights you've gained, and the progress you've made are all part of a foundation that will serve you for years to come. Remember, mastery isn't the end—it's a new beginning. Use what you've learned to tackle bigger challenges, inspire others, and continue growing into the best version of yourself.

29
CELEBRATE AND PLAN AHEAD

You did it! You've completed an incredible 90-day journey—one that's transformed not just your skill but your entire mindset.

I still remember the day I completed my first 90-day challenge. I looked back at my progress with a mix of pride and disbelief. The confidence I gained wasn't just from mastering a skill—it was from proving to myself that I could stick with something, adapt, and grow. That feeling changed everything for me.

This isn't just about crossing a finish line. It's about realizing your potential and proving to yourself what's possible when you commit, stay focused, and take consistent action. This chapter is your moment to pause, celebrate, and reflect on everything you've accomplished. But let's be honest—this is just the beginning. You've built the momentum; now it's time to keep it going.

Reflect

Reflection turns effort into insight. It helps you recognize your wins, learn from the process, and prepare for your next growth journey.

How Do You Feel?

Take a moment to reflect on how you've grown over the past 90 days.

What moments stand out? Was it overcoming a tough challenge, receiving positive feedback, or simply realizing you were capable of more than you imagined?

What Was the Most Valuable Lesson?

Identify the one thing that made the biggest difference in your journey. Was it a strategy, a skill, or a mindset shift?

What Progress Are You Most Proud Of?

Celebrate your wins! What milestones make you feel unstoppable? Recognize and honor the hard work that got you here.

How Has Your Confidence Grown?

Think about how far you've come. Are you approaching challenges with a new mindset? How has this journey reshaped your belief in what you can achieve?

Your story is powerful. Share it with others in your network or community to inspire and celebrate together.

Empower

Your growth isn't just for you—it's a chance to inspire others. By sharing your journey, you can help others believe in their potential.

Inspire Others Through Honesty

Be real about the challenges you faced and how you overcame them. Your honesty shows others that growth isn't always easy—but it's always worth it.

Fuel Collective Growth

Your success can ignite someone else's journey. Every tip you share or milestone you celebrate adds value to your community. Consider hosting a mini-session or sharing a guide to help others start their own 90-day journey. When you give back, you amplify the impact of your growth.

Plan Ahead

This isn't the end—it's the beginning of your next chapter. What's the next skill you want to conquer?

What's the Next Skill?

Think about a skill that will take you further in your career or personal growth. What's the next challenge that excites you?

Build Momentum

Each 90-day cycle builds on the last. With every success, you gain confidence and energy to tackle bigger goals. Where could this momentum take you?

Closing Thought

You've accomplished something incredible. Not just because you mastered a skill, but because you proved to yourself that growth is always within reach. The 90-day framework isn't just a tool—it's a mindset. It's your strategy for staying ahead, adapting to change, and pursuing greatness.

Thank you for being part of this journey. Now, go celebrate—you've earned it! And when you're ready, your next challenge will be waiting.   Let's   keep   climbing!

ABOUT THE AUTHOR

Dan Clapper is a lifelong champion of personal and professional growth, dedicated to helping individuals unlock their potential and master transformative skills. With over 25 years of experience spanning training, talent development, and hands-on industry expertise, Dan has guided countless professionals to rise to the top of their fields.

As the Head of Learner and Business Outcomes at Interplay Learning, Dan leverages his Certified Professional in Talent Development (CPTD) credential to design cutting-edge training programs that create career opportunities and drive measurable business success. From installing boilers and HVAC equipment as a teenager with his father to coaching trade professionals across the country, Dan's journey has been as hands-on as it is inspiring.

Dan is also the founder of the Top 10% Club, a vibrant community where ambitious professionals collaborate, grow, and succeed together. To make the Top 10% Club more accessible, Dan developed a mobile app available for both Apple and Android devices, offering tools, resources, and connections to help users achieve their career goals.

An author, speaker, and podcast guest, Dan is passionate about sharing his insights on career development and talent optimization.

Want to connect with Dan? He's always open to podcasts, speaking engagements, webinars, and more. Email him at Dan@top10percentclub.com—he'd love to hear from you!

Special Offer for Book Readers: Take Your Learning and Peer Network to the Next Level!

Congratulations on investing in your growth by reading Master a Career-Defining Skill in 90 Days! If you're ready to transform your career even further, we've got an exclusive opportunity just for you.

Introducing the Master a Career-Defining Skill Online Course

The book gives you the framework—now experience the transformation! Our online course brings the concepts in this book to life through dynamic video lessons, interactive tools, and an engaged community of growth-minded professionals.

Includes membership to the Top 10% Club, an exclusive online community of peers and mentors!

Get feedback, brainstorm ideas, and celebrate your wins with like-minded professionals.   Accessible via Mobile App and Desktop!

Your Exclusive Discount

As a valued reader of this book, you get a special discount code to join the course. Use code **BOOK75** at checkout to save 75% on the course price—just $99 (regularly $399)!

Here's How to Get Started:

Visit https://top10percentclub/bookdeal

Enter the code **BOOK75** during checkout.

This special offer is only available to book readers. Act now to take advantage of this exclusive opportunity!

Made in the USA
Monee, IL
10 January 2025

76467819R00085